PRAISE FOR
MELLARA GOLD'S 2021 BOOK
A LIFE WORTH LIVING

A Life Worth Living is a book worth reading. Not only could I relate to many of the author's struggles, but also experienced a deep curiosity growing in me as I followed the stages of her transformational spiritual journey. Where would she take me next? This is not a book written with objectivity. It is the exact opposite. *A Life Worth Living* is written with a passion and fierceness that is the perfect antidote to any cool, above-it-all preaching about what happens when we commit ourselves to the path of yoga. I will gratefully carry the words of this Warrior-Princess-Seeker with me as I continue my own spiritual journey, feeling a little less lonely, a little less afraid, and a lot more inspired. Join us.

> — **Judith Hanson Lasater**, PhD, PT, international yoga teacher since 1971, author of 11 books, most recently *Teaching Yoga with Intention: The Essential Guide to Skillful Hands-on Assists and Verbal Communication*

Mellara's book dives deep into the passage of yoga and how we can use our practice (yoga), our breath, and our awareness to create more love and peace in our lives. I see so much of my own journey in Mellara's and suspect many others will relate to her journey as well.

> — **Mariel Hemingway**, actress and author of *Out Came the Sun*

A Life Worth Living is one woman's story of struggle, redemption, and deep learning. Mellara shows us how healing is possible through presence, devotion, and practical listening.

> — **Elena Brower**, author of *Being You* & other bestselling titles, and podcast host of *Practice You*

Mellara's love shines in her words of wisdom and practical Dharma teachings throughout *A Life Worth Living*. As she shares her journey with us, she sprinkles the path with supportive spiritual reminders that this life is precious and we can find inspiration and healing during even the most arduous moments. Keep this book by your side in these unsettling times!

> — **Núbia Teixeira**, author of *Yoga and the Art of Mudras,* Founder of Bhakti Nova School of Yoga, Dance & Reiki, and of "Nubia's Devotional Yoga Online School" on Patreon

A Life Worth Living is a spiritual memoir of awakening that is raw, brave, and universally touching. As she shares her engaging and often heart-wrenching journey, Mellara's spirit rises time and again to reach for the light. Her book inspires, gently guides, and humbly reveals her own struggles and commitment to a path that she has mastered through honesty, love, and perseverance. To read this book is to experience a shift, not through instruction necessarily, but through absorption of the transmission of energy that Mellara is offering page by page. This book is a powerful and effective meditation on love and resilience.

> — **Christine Burke**, author of *The Yoga Healer* and *The Power of Breath and Hand Yoga* and owner of Liberation Yoga Studio in Los Angeles

In this wonderful memoir and manual of yogic practice, Mellara brings us humbly and deftly into her experience, and in so doing into our own—and we come out the other end changed for the better. Mellara's love, light, and beauty can be felt in every word.

> — **Melanie Salvatore-August**, author of *Fierce Kindness* and *Yoga to Support Immunity*

LIVING IN AWARENESS

Deepening Our Daily Lives Through Prayer, Ritual, and Meditation

by Mellara Gold, author of
A Life Worth Living

Illustrations by Leela Anzenberger

MANDORLA BOOKS
WWW.MANDORLABOOKS.COM

I would like to dedicate this book to all sensitive, undeniably human and sentient beings.

To all of us spirits having this sometimes wild and crazy human experience....

you are loved and this book is for you, dear one.

Table of Contents

INTRODUCTION

"Now when I sit quietly, I ask myself, 'Who am I? Who is carrying this body?' The answer is not my identity, gender, or thoughts, but what I'm feeling and sensing inside."
— from *A Life Worth Living*

Living in awareness is about living more deeply and with mindful attention to the life that we are co-creating with the universe. It might even be considered a way to be with our inner life more consciously. Our perspective is essentially how we "see" the world. I see you, my dear readers, from my own lens based on my experiences, and I write from that lens as well. I can only offer what I know, what I've seen, what I've felt to be true, and hope it will be of value to you. So please, take what resonates with you in this book and leave the rest in the pages of my heart. Only you can really know what you need in your life.

I started practicing yoga positions, or *asanas*, in the mid-'90s and began my teaching journey shortly after that. Before practicing, I remember feeling old in a young person's body: I had just been diagnosed with five bulging discs. The pain and discomfort in my body led me onto a path of self-healing. After the crying and pity party subsided, I began to show up consistently to yoga classes, and finally, I found relief. It was a mind, body, and soul relief. In practicing yoga, I found that a lot of my pain subsided in conjunction with a combination of acupuncture treatments. I became more aware of my inner life, something I hadn't previously been good at noticing at all. As a child, I had a healthy inner life and was also good at disassociating from my body and running away from the truth of my feelings. As a sensitive child, I remember wishing there was a pill I could take to get rid of my tendency to over-feel. Now, as a 47-year-old woman, I know that my sensitivity and my ability to be vulnerable is, and has ironically always been, my superpower.

When I was given pain pills at the onset of my back diagnosis, I loved the feeling of numbing out. As a result, my life felt uninteresting and non-productive. As yoga became my world, I came to realize that I couldn't go on like that. Instead of taking the pain pills, I'd go to one, sometimes two, yoga classes a day. I also noticed that some of my external life difficulties eased up, but mostly, my mental and physical health was improving, even if just a little. Prior to this, I was always getting into trouble, especially as a young, fresh-faced Australian actress living in Hollywood. Or was it that trouble was always finding me? Probably a bit of both—as Rumi has famously told us, what we seek is seeking us. Sadly, I was unconsciously a magnet for the negative energy I was feeling within me, drawing negative energy to myself. But yoga continued to be my constant refuge, and teaching yoga became a natural next step.

A regular meditation practice and learning to live in awareness would come much later in my life. These were both natural progressions in a life worth living. As I studied with different yoga teachers and healers along the way, I began to notice that I would give my power away to them. Without much self-esteem, I felt that they had all the answers to my questions. If I could just be at their feet, the transmission of their knowledge would flood into me, I believed. What I didn't realize was that I was leaking energy and giving my power to others when the messages of inner peace and love were inside me all along. Through yoga, my body began to remind me that I matter, that my feelings matter. I longed to bring what I was learning in my yoga poses into the life I was living, yet I fell short. Eventually there was nowhere to go but to let go—I had reached so many rock bottoms that I felt like a cat with nine lives, waiting for peace. All the yoga, therapy, and work of inner reflection began to make their mark on me as I got closer to 40.

When my kids, husband, and I moved from California back to my native country Australia in 2015, I had already been a yoga teacher for

18 years. I continued to work on mindfulness, yoga, and studying Buddhist teachings in Australia. I did so in a more methodical way with yoga teacher, author, and monastically-trained Buddhist upāsaka Channa Dassanayaka. I think that the universe conspired to bring me the perfect teacher at the perfect time in my life—when I was ready to finally come home to myself. I'm so grateful for my time with Channa for so many reasons, but mostly because it helped me to soften, be less hard on myself, and become more self-compassionate. I wrote about my experience with Channa in my first book, *A Life Worth Living: A Journey of Self-Discovery Through Mindfulness, Yoga, and Living in Awareness.*

Even though I was learning and discovering so much, and I thought that I healed my wounds, when we returned to the States in the summer of 2016, I still didn't completely trust in myself. I was still relying on reassurance and guidance from Channa, yet now it happened on the phone and not in person.

Eventually, as I wrote about in more detail in *A Live Worth Living*, I realized it was time for me to stand on my own two feet and truly embody being my own best teacher, guide, and parent. I wasn't alone—I had my friends, family, students, and children around me—yet somehow, I still felt lonely. This was just before the pandemic hit, and I realized that I was on a spiritual journey like nothing I had ever experienced. I used the isolation period to do the healing that I needed, spending a lot of time self-reflecting between teaching yoga, playing with Rosie, our beloved dog, caring for my children, and running the household. I think my husband must have known what I was going through, yet he never said much about it. Perhaps that's because he knew it was up to me to work through my emotions, grief, and pain. I knew that a newfound distance from Channa was just what I needed to stop looking on the outside for someone else to validate my existence, to give me the kind of love, support, and guidance I never experienced from my parents. I soon came to realize that this kind of "leveling up," if you will, has always been a solo act. I knew I had to journey it alone. Without spoiling the ending for you, it was all worth it!

This time of aloneness and healing reminded me of something Albert Einstein said: "Although I am a typical loner in my daily life, my awareness of belonging to the invisible community of those who strive for truth, beauty and justice has prevented me from feelings of isolation." I eventually got to that place of awareness that Einstein speaks of, and it was profoundly healing to realize that I wasn't alone after all. Even in the pandemic's isolation, I was part of a community of people seeking to live a life of awareness. It is for this community— *it is for you*—that I offer this book.

This book is the result of decades of my ongoing personal exploration, my work with students and colleagues, and my life with my family and friends. The world around us is changing so rapidly and these are potent times for inner transformation. My hope is that this book might meet you where you are in your healing journey and, like a mighty river, provide you with some inspiration along the way. It is written from my heart to yours.

This book is for the community of people who would like to live with more clarity, love, and self-compassion through our long, windy journey called life. I invite you to join me in a spiritual and mindful dance with an open heart, full of love and grace. I offer this profoundly compassionate alternative way of living, one where we live an embodied life, honoring messages from the body, emotions, and heart, while also integrating the mind. Together, we will explore what a home practice might look like, and how it can help us have a deeper, more conscious relationship with ourselves, others, and Mother Earth. I have also included specific questions for you to reflect upon, because the focus of this book is not only on the practices of yoga, prayer, or mindful breathing: I believe that increased awareness is possible in all areas of our life. The question is, how can we live our daily lives with awareness, presence, and satisfaction?

I've come to believe that the first step is to listen with awareness to ourselves and others while caring deeply for our bodies and the Earth. As we develop practices that reveal our inner truths, we can let these truths permeate all of existence. These are the changes needed today, and they can begin in our inner sanctums.

The things in our life that tend to bring us the most excitement, peace, and joy are like bridges to a place within us that shows us we're headed in the right direction. Through our everyday dedication to lifestyles that support bridge-making, our life begins to take shape in ways that please us, that afford us more of our own precious inner peace.

In this book, you will find suggestions on how to do just that. From the way we look after ourselves in the morning to how we approach the end of our evenings, everything we do with awareness makes a difference. Creating small and attainable changes in our lives means we are improving our lives with consistency, no matter what amount of time we can give to it. When you find ideas and practices in this book that resonate with you, try to implement them a little every day, even if only for a few minutes.

As we come to the end of this introduction, I have a suggestion for you. For a few moments, maybe close your eyes, take a deep breath in, and feel that untouched place within you that has never been hurt or betrayed. You may have lived a difficult life since your birth, and can't access that untouched place in this lifetime, but see if you can access a time before this lifetime when your soul was pure peace and love. Stay there and connect with the truest understanding of who you are. Exhale into the softer part of you and the gentleness within that brings us into connection with the whole of the cosmos. This awareness takes some practice. Think of it like learning to paddleboard in the summertime: if you're not dedicating time to it regularly, it is almost impossible to feel its benefits. But soon enough, you will be standing proud and tall, paddling through the water.

Here is an affirmation to celebrate the life you are living:

I am so in love with life itself. I am becoming wiser. I am safe. I am strong. I am sovereign. I feel blessings with each breath that breathes me. I'm so eager about my life. I feel stable, and I feel secure. My heart is full of love and it's a joy to be me and be around me.

Lots of love,
Mellara

Publisher's Note: These graphics will help you locate Mellara's offerings of prayers, rituals, and meditations

     Prayers

     Rituals

     Meditations

PRACTICING WITH AWARENESS

"We can't solve a problem with the same mind that created it."
— **Albert Einstein**

I'd love to start this chapter by laying a foundation regarding the subtle mind, the mind within the mind. According to yogic understanding, there are four parts of our mind: *Buddhi, Manas, Ahankara, and Chitta.* Inside these parts of our mind are where we might ask questions like, "Who might I be without my story or my roles in life?" Sometimes when I'm nearing the end of meditation, I like to ask myself this. Not getting an answer for me feels okay too. Being with the question might be enough to stretch that part of our mind toward something more expansive and free. Below are the four parts of the mind that I'm excited to share with you—or maybe you've already heard of them, in which case this will be a reminder. Could you perhaps, after reading this section, sit in a chair and gently place your feet on the ground, close your eyes, and begin by asking yourself

Mind - *Is this who I am?*

Buddhi is the part of our minds we use mostly in our daily lives. We've been trained from an early age to do so—our school systems emphasize the cultivation of the Buddhi part of our minds. It's as though the more we can memorize, the fuller our memory becomes, and the more we put this into practice in the form of tests and exams, then the stronger our buddhi. This is only one way to tap into the full potential of who we are. If we "see" this through our understanding and insight, we could think it silly to focus only on this one part of ourselves.

When we practice exercising this part of our mind again and again, the it functions better. This is what I believe is known as "intelligence" today, which is different from wisdom, or understanding our emotions and energy. Still, intelligence has its value. The quicker your mind, the more you can speak on a subject. The more you have to say with your intelligent mind, the more you, and what you have to say, is applauded. Being "smart" is one of our must-haves in today's world, which isn't, of course, a bad thing, but perhaps we can expand our minds in different ways as well. By practicing meditation, we can tap into a deeper way of existence that goes beyond only using our buddhi or intellect.

Manas is the next dimension of our mind. From the top of our heads down to our toes, we have what is known as our body's intelligence.

Science is showing us that every cell in the body has a phenomenal memory, and through the current field of epigenetics, we're learning that our ancestors live inside of us too—not just their spirits, but their bodies have left behind their intelligence in our very DNA. Their wounds leave traces in our bodies as well. Tara Brach, a meditation teacher and the author of *Racial Compassion*, has said, "Our issues are in our tissues." The implications of this new science into the body's intelligence are mind-blowing. It means that if we're working on healing ourselves, altering our own genetic markers, we are supporting the healing of our descendants, the ones who will inherit our bodily intelligence. Spiritual teachers have also suggested it works in reverse, that when we heal ourselves, we heal our ancestral line as well—see Daniel Foor's book *Ancestral Medicine: Rituals for Personal and Family Healing* as one example.

Without combining or bringing together in harmony our Buddhi and Manas (brain and body awareness), we are left feeling more stressed than we have ever been, and disconnected from ourselves. Our spiritual practices are best when we include the body, as it holds a much deeper understanding of who we are.

The third part of the mind's optimal potential is **Ahankara**, or our sense of identity. According to spiritual teacher Sadhguru Jaggi Vasudev, Ahankara "is sometimes translated as ego, but it is much more than that." Another translation is that it's the "I-making" function of the mind. What I've learned from yogic teachings is that once our sense of identity is known to us, our intellect can only function from that context, from the "I." Therefore, we have an important opportunity to inquire inside ourselves and ponder how we might be much more than our roles in life, those roles our egos have chosen in life, those identities we've chosen to align ourselves with. Belonging to a certain nation, community, group, gender, and whatever else we identify with is of course important for our survival, but in the end, is it all of who we are? How can we cultivate more expansive identities, expanding this third part of our mind?

Chitta, or cosmic intelligence, according to Sadhguru Jaggi Vasudev, is the "pure intelligence" that occurs in the background of our minds even if we aren't aware of it. It's the part of our mind that keeps us alive, making our life happen, but we may not be conscious of it. We don't necessarily know how we know to get up and go to the bathroom when we must go, but we do. Chitta is a deep intelligence at play that invites us to be with all of life. We might go a little crazy trying to understand how everything is working in our lives, the cosmic significance of what is happening with us and to us, so sometimes it is better to just be with it, to go with the flow. When we are tapped into Chitta, then God, Divine Energy, or the Universe (whatever your name for it) is working *through* us, *with* us, and *as* us, and we might say that we feel connected not only to ourselves but to all things in a conscious way. It might be likened to the saying "Let Go and Let God," which means to let go of desired outcomes and allow for the divine energy within us to manifest what is best for us while getting out of the way of our limited ego consciousness.

When Chitta is easily flowing and our physical conditions seem to be, for the most part, taken care of, we have more time to look within and deepen our connection to ourselves. We don't need to consume more—when we let go and let God, we are unconditionally satisfied with who we are already and what we have. When we're in our Chitta mind, we regularly give time to ourselves, strengthening the

connection we have with ourselves and with those around us. You'll
know when you have felt the energy of Chitta inside of you because
everything will just seem to flow more effortlessly in the now of your
life. There isn't a memory of what once was, there is a much bigger
perspective where decisions are made from the horizon of our mind,
body, identity, and beingness.

Another way to strengthen our connection to Chitta and our other
three minds is to recognize ourselves in those first few moments when
we wake from sleep and we are in that wake/dream state of awareness.
This space reminds us that no matter what kind of stressors are happening in life, in this moment, this feeling could just be the closest
feeling to who we really are.

So let's recap. If I am not my child who is recovering from a basketball
injury asleep in the other room, nor am I my husband's work stressors,
nor am I a grieving dog mom of her five-year-old pup who just passed
away from leukemia, then who and what is me? These are very real
things happening in my life, but does it make me who I am, and why
might it matter anyway? In the physical, human sense, they absolutely
matter. Anything that has come our way shapes us into the personali-
ties of who we are. But if we define our lives only from what is happening in the external world, much of which we have no control over
anyway, we are almost always going to fall short. This doesn't mean
that we don't strive for certain things that we would like out of life—
we still can and do—but if we close our eyes for a moment and feel
the presence of who we are while sitting in the quietness, we might
recognize that our roles and any unhealthy states of mind or urges do
not need to define us. We all have roles and responsibilities, but perhaps we don't have to feel as if they need to make up the total sum of
who we are. Nor do we always have to feel as if we are fighting our
way through life every day. There is nothing wrong if we are—after all,
we are human beings in a body just doing the best we can. But remember that the possibility for a more peaceful life inside busyness and
stressful roles in life is possible. We can rely on our Chitta mind that
lives inside us, the deeper part of us that knows its cosmic connection
with ourselves and all of life.

As a meditation teacher, I sometimes hold a bell in my hand. As a curious teacher and student, I'm pretty sure the bell is not me. It may be something I'm holding in my hand, but it's not me. This example is much easier to understand because we can physically see the bell as a "thing" outside of me. But what about the clothes we wear? Does that make us who we are? What about our mathematical intelligence, or our ability to write beautiful music? Does that define who we are? Or how about the car we drive or our other possessions? How about when we chip a fingernail, and it falls on the kitchen counter, is that nail us? Is our hair an identification of the self? Is the kidney the self? Are our eyelashes the self? What about the ear canal? Our true self is probably not any of these things.

As the mind gets quieter and quieter and more concentrated, we have the opportunity to see what is not us, what slows up the mind, and where we lose our understanding of the magnificent whole of who we really are. Sometimes I'll get caught up in assuming that I am one of these external things, and it's mostly unconscious. For example, it can be something as small as having a bad hair day. If I'm not aware of my negative thoughts about my hair's appearance, I may end up having an awful day just because I'm associating my hair with who I am as a person. And when this happens, and I anchor into thinking that I am only something outside of myself, I feel a slight degree of agitation or tightness in me.

Let's take my daughter as another example. In my more enlightened moments, I consider her to be "a" daughter; she is not me, mine, or an extension of me, she is merely another human being that I am privileged to walk alongside and just happen to be responsible for while she's young. She does not make me who I am, yet I play an important role as her mother. The experiences of being with her are valuable. My role as her mother is such a huge teacher for me, but from a spiritual perspective, it is not all of who I am.

I certainly don't have it all figured out, and like most of us, I am a work in progress, but what works for me is knowing that I am supported by my roles rather than ruled by them. And while you certainly don't need to take my word for it, you might explore this understanding within your own body, spirit, and mind. I also have a prayer for us.

May we surrender into other aspects of who we are, be it the "being" part of our humanness and not only our personality or our appearance, but the space between those things where we are inspired by our truest form of beingness.

When we identify ourselves by only our personality or our appearance, and we feel resistance to our appearance changing especially as we age, we tend to feel bad about ourselves. I remember a day when I showed up to class to teach yoga and I had just cracked my front tooth from biting into an apple. I was horrified and thought for a second, who am I without my perfect smile? How will other people see that person? And I realized that my worth was attached to or wrapped around my physical appearance much more than I had imagined. It developed unconsciously in the beginning, where over the years I was identifying with having a beautiful smile. Because I had associated my sense of self with my smile, I suffered when I went to class that day with a cracked tooth, feeling flawed and unworthy. So silly, right? Yet so very human.

If I could have simply "owned" my physical flaw in that moment without believing that it made me who I am, I probably would have kept calm (within) and carried on. To this day, I still remember not feeling like I was enough with this "imperfection." If only I could have just loved myself in that moment, all of me, including the so-called flaw of my tooth, and visited the untouched place within me that has never been hurt, rejected, or betrayed, perhaps then I might have felt okay about teaching class that day and not felt so self-conscious. If only I could have moved into an acceptance of myself with a huge crack in my tooth, until it eventually got restored. If we define ourselves by external things such as our smile, then it doesn't allow each moment to be "as it is," nor does it allow us to "be as we are." This is especially important as we age, as who we are on the outside inevitably changes. It's essential that we regularly practice letting go of what we physically once were and allow impermanence a place to sit in our hearts. To that end, I have another prayer for us.

May we let go of who we thought we were before supposed big bad things happened to us. If you are a parent, allow the next generation the space to grow into who they feel themselves to be. To be in communion with our beautiful and so-called flawed body is to have a "wholeness" mindset, to include it all—not just the pretty parts of our body or personality, but to love it all. And in this understanding, we see that in letting go, we restore the power back to ourselves and enjoy each moment as our lives unfold.

I have found it to be a slow process of looking into and feeling what I may not need to identify with anymore. It simply becomes a practice like anything else that's important to us. Remember that practice makes progress, and it doesn't need to look a particular way for its benefits to be felt.

MEDITATION: TO NOT BE THE BODY

Body - *Is this who I am?*

You might already have a meditation practice of your own but are you open to trying something different today? Could you find a place where you won't be disturbed and where you might sit or lie down? Let's meditate on what it might feel like not to be the body or anything else on the outside of our beingness or spirit nature.

This can have a profound effect on us as we step out from our rational minds with their identities and into a more spacious awareness, the space that sits like the blue sky behind the clouds.

Bring your awareness to your third eye, that little space between your two eyes. Visualize the feeling of having a real eye there—that is where the opening to our insight lives. Wait for a moment until you experience who you really are. Allow whatever arises to arise. Nothing is right or wrong, so just practice.

As you step into the wide-open space of who you are beyond your physical form, be open to any shapes or colors that you might see. Instead of "looking" for anything, just be with what is there and open yourself up to gently receiving.

The grace and depth of who we are is always eagerly waiting for us to recognize it and be with it in awareness. The eye or I-ness (awareness state) of who we are might be considered our truest self—let's call it the "subject." The body can be called the "object" living just outside of the beingness of our subject. Please say hello to this part of you and sit for as long as you would like. Perhaps set a timer for five minutes.

Now with this understanding, say out loud, even if only as a whisper, "I am not my body." Our bodies are an object that carries us where we need to go, and they allow us to experience life through the senses, to have bodily intelligence, yet they are not all of who we are. Now repeat after me, "I am not my organs." Our organs are incredible and especially how they just go on working in the background, doing such important work, yet they are not all of who we are. Now move your awareness down to your feet and slowly move up from the body, repeating with feeling and emphasis each body part, and continue. "Am I my toenails?" "Am I my ankles?" "Am I my shin bone, left and right side?" "Am I my knee bones, left and right side?" "Am I my thighs, left and right side?" "Am I my pelvic floor?" "Am I my hip, left and right side?" "Am I my stomach?" "Am I my heart?" "Am I my shoulders or any pain I might be feeling inside them, left and right side?" "Am I my jaw, nose, eyes, or ears?"

Now we can move further outside of ourselves and continue to inquire inside. "Is my daughter mine?" "Is my son mine?" "Is my partner, house, car, holiday and kitchen really mine?" Or are they just what they are? Continue like this and make it personal for you, adding in what you feel you might want to inquire about, that which you've come to identify with. It can be quite freeing to work with loving all of what makes us who we are while simultaneously not feeling owned or that we own the things in our life and outside of it. May we feel a deep belonging to ourselves and be grateful for the gift of "seeing" (with our insight) who we really are.

So, what might be given to us if and when we see the benefits of this understanding? How does this help us in our very busy and sometimes crazy modern life? Everyone will benefit in different ways, but what I've heard most folks say is that they feel more engaged in their life rather than bogged down by it. Everything changes; we live in an impermanent world, and we go back into the divine consciousness the very same way in which we came in, being nothing, and taking nothing with us.

Sometimes I've heard spiritual folks take this a step further by saying, "There is no self," but while I can feel some truth in this statement, it can be quite confusing. What do we really mean by "there is no self?" Because here I am, standing or sitting, and feeling very much alive and present. And if there's no self, then who's needing food or who's needing to have a nap? It's not really a statement of "no self," but it's more about how we identify or define the self.

Let's not make this too complicated or confusing, or we'll lose the whole point of the practice. It's rather easy—think of it as just getting quiet and realizing, "Wow, I didn't even know how much I am identified with 'x' [whatever it is for you that you might be identified with]." For me, it was, and sometimes still is, my physical appearance, and how I'd like to look a certain way. But I know that my appearance will continue to change, and I try to remember that everything in life is changing. If we don't allow things to change, or double down and actively block those changes, then we'll end up feeling more unsettled inside. I don't think there is any crime in wanting to look well put-together; it's the wish that our outer appearance [or whatever your "x" may be] remains the same that we feel a disconnect.

Sometimes, I can be looking at my teens at the dinner table and find that I'm experiencing a moment of love as a few tears fill up my eyes and beingness. I'm not sad really, it's more like a bittersweet feeling of how precious (and sometimes challenging) these moments with them are, knowing that someday they will be out of my house, living their own lives. In these moments, I try to remind myself that I'm raising my children to be their own persons, and while that doesn't mean that I will be necessarily separate from them, it just means that things change. On these occasions, I am comforted by the present moment, and remind myself that simply being with them is the gift. Again, we live in an impermanent world, and as much as we might like time to stop, only change remains the same.

It's not just physical attributes or possessions that we identify with that can cause us to suffer, but lingering emotions as well. My past anger isn't who I am either—thinking about that only makes me feel bad, most especially if I identify with it, and with being an angry person. This realization often comes gradually to me. One day I'll be going about my day and notice that I'm still holding onto that anger. If I can interrupt this thought—with a breathing exercise, or walk, or shower meditation—perhaps I can see that I don't need to hold onto it anymore. I can see that when I'm still angry at myself or someone that I might be able to still love, and at the same time I don't have to be okay with their actions or even like them. When I remember to do this, I feel more at peace inside.

Living in awareness doesn't mean we won't ever go back to these past versions of how we identified, it's just that they don't have to stay for an overnight visit like they once did. This can help us to feel freer in our human existence and in the roles we are taking on to complete our soul's purpose in this lifetime.

May we include the physical body inside our spiritual practice as the temple that it is.

OUR FIRST HOME: OUR BODY

Let's continue our practice of awareness by looking at our first home: our body. We might agree that our body is a profound vehicle for transformation. From an early age, we are often called upon to bear witness and live through the unbearable, starting with our very birth.

Unfortunately, a lot of us face some degree of trauma in our lifetime, from our families, from our time in school, from our religion, from our society. Even the most loving of families with the best of intentions can't keep us from experiencing some forms of trauma. Life-changing events such as divorce, death, natural disasters, and being victims of crime or of war, all impact us in different ways. Sometimes, unconsciously, we also perpetuate generational and developmental trauma ourselves. Exciting developments in science are showing how our trauma lives on in our bodies (post-traumatic stress disorder, for example), something I know first-hand from my experience as a yoga teacher and a trauma survivor.

One day, when I was teaching a yoga class, I could feel the energy in the room building, almost like a release was just waiting to happen. Was it with me, or was it with my students? I wasn't sure. Perhaps it was a bit of both. We were in the middle of our practice, and I knew we needed a song to move to, to dance to. I put on a slow dance song, "Diamonds in The Sun" with Girish, Donna De Lory, Hans Christian, Mario Abney, and Jeremy Ruzumna, a song that we could move to individually on our 2x4 piece of yoga mat. The song includes *Lokah Samastah Sukhino*, a mantra we use a lot in our yoga community. It basically means, *May the entire world be happy.*

I can't speak for the others, but I could feel a part of me was coming up to the surface, ready for healing. Through the gentle movement of my body and with these words, I connected to a place inside where I sometimes don't feel worthy of my own love. As we got to the part in the song where it says that we are all diamonds in the sun, and we all shine, I felt these happy tears of release in the company of my beloved friends and students.

I'm not sure what happened that day, but it was beautiful, and I noticed that I wasn't the only one weeping. We paused for a bit, became aware of our breath after, and stood still for a moment in the silence, feeling what had just transpired. It was such a powerful moment. It felt like a gift to be able to move through what was happening in a safe and supportive environment. A week later, one student mentioned that because of that class, she saw that she could give herself the love she never received from her mother. Although she received that love from others in her life, she said she didn't need it to feel validated in her own skin like she did with her mother's love. She went on to say that being able to give herself the love she didn't receive from her mother wasn't a feeling, but a real knowing in her heart.

All of us have a body inside of the body. In this very moment, close your eyes and begin to feel yours with one conscious breath in, and one conscious breath out. It's an invisible body if you will, the energy or essence of who you are. Take a moment to pause and remember that you are meant to be here, you matter, and everything that has happened to you and for you has brought you to this moment. We don't continue the path of healing because we are not already whole; we continue a healing journey in order to remember our wholeness and who we really are.

May we, on a regular basis, tap into our inner world throughout the span of one day.

While tapping in like this doesn't need to be complicated or made into a big deal, it is an intention you can set for the day. If you have access to the outdoors, go walk on the grass and feel the cool dew or warm grass under your feet. Recite a mantra that comes to you naturally like *I am walking on this grass* or *I can feel Mother Gaia's love running through me*. When we do a simple exercise like this, it helps us to remember the gentleness of who we are, our beingness. Being with Mother Nature helps us to connect with the god or universal love of our own understanding and truest nature. And just by observing the external body, we can feel that we have an internal body too. At the center of our being, we can settle in and be with our true self, just like a marble that is placed in a bowl and slowly makes its way to the center.

MEDITATION: A JOURNEY INTO OUR CENTER

Let's take a journey to our center. In the practice of feeling centered, we can start right where we are. Whatever emotions, body sensations, or life situations that are happening in this moment, let's be this feeling and start our marble at the high side of a bowl. Just like the world we are living in, so too do we have a perfectly rounded bowl. Now, place the marble in the bowl and release it. You are the marble. Now observe within you that your body, the marble, rolls down to the bottom again and rolls up to the starting position. The marble continues to oscillate. This is not unlike how we are inside one day, a week, a month, or years. Eventually, just like the marble, we make our way to the center. When we are in the midst of uncertainty, engulfed in grief or fear, it is hard to imagine things changing. Perhaps we can take some comfort in knowing that everything is a temporary oscillation until we come again to center. Perhaps the simple "shedding of light" onto this understanding can be the medicine for the transformation taking place within and outside of us too.

Our tendency is to get distracted and wander off with thought, but this won't happen if we follow the marble to its home into the depth of our being, into the center. As we practice holding our mindful attention, our mind does eventually find rest, which is our present-moment awareness. Once the marble of our awareness settles at the bottom of the bowl, we are not going back and forth from past experiences and future thoughts. We are merely settled inside the bowl where we can observe freely while also relaxing into beingness. We are not *for* anything, nor *against* anything, nor *entangled in* anything; we are simply present. Each moment has its own completeness or energy.

 Perhaps in this moment open yourself up to deeper listening as if every sound is moving toward you. You are the center; you are the universe and all sounds come from every direction to you. Close your eyes and feel sound all around you. It's the focus of your listening that matters most and not so much what you're listening to, whether that's the sound of the imaginary marble in our inner listening, or the sound of the traffic outside our home or a dog barking in the neighborhood. Just relax into the nothingness of everything that is happening. Inside of inner silence, everything and nothing is happening all at once. This is a meditation where a mundane, yet sacred,

experience is being born, and it is a wonderful practice to do when we are not feeling settled inside.

Let's sit in a chair, firmly yet gently place your feet on the ground, close your eyes, and begin by asking…

Spirit - *Is this who I am?*

MEDITATION: CONNECTING THE SPIRIT AND THE BODY

Follow the breath, dear one, as it is the bridge that brings us to our beingness, to our essential spirit nature.

 To help us cross this bridge that connects our bodies to our essential spirit nature, let's practice conscious breathing for three minutes. Perhaps you already have a similar way to connect with your breath. This is one of the simplest yet effective ways to allow our being or spirit nature to be felt. I learned this meditation practice from Ram Dass.

Please lay down or sit tall with your spine long, either cross-legged or up on your knees, perhaps sitting on two yoga blocks. You may also sit down in a chair. Now place your hands on your belly just below your rib cage. Begin by noticing that as you take a breath in, your belly rises just below your rib cage. As you breathe in, belly rises; as you breathe out, belly falls. The key instruction is to not attend to the breath as much as it is to observe the belly rising and falling. For the next three minutes, belly is rising, and belly is falling. As we do this, may we let go of trying to determine if this is working and simply be with the rising and falling of the belly. Let go of any judgments about whether you might be doing this right, and just attend to the belly rising and falling. When distractions come in, allow them, but stay focused on the belly rising and falling. And when you feel your belly rising, see it within you rising. When you feel it falling, see it also within you falling.

If you have a timer at home, set it now for three or more minutes, and notice if there has been a gentle energy shift within you.

RITUALS AND MEDITATIONS FOR CONNECTING WITH THE SPIRIT WITHIN

There are many other ways to connect with the spirit within. Sometimes when I am not feeling connected to my true self, or spirit as I like to call it, there are a few things that help me get there.

 One of them is opening the window to breathe in some fresh air while closing and opening my eyes, back and forth. When the eyes are open, we might gaze at the sky and see the clouds and the light around them. Our inner refuge is merely a breath away as we expose ourselves to the outer sky and environment. Close your eyes and breathe in the spaciousness that is waiting for you.

Or you might rest with your eyes open for five or ten minutes at a time just watching the sky be the sky, simply looking at the sky, light, and clouds, doing nothing else at all. Try not to be pulled in by the mind as it might distract you into thinking that your phone, a notification, or anything in your house might need to be taken care of at that moment. For ten or so minutes, allow yourself to have this time completely as a support for connecting with your inner spaciousness. All your cares and worries will still be there after the ten minutes, but your perspective around them may have changed. May we remember that our true nature is open and clear like the sky and is only temporarily blocked by the clouds of any mild anxiety and depression.

Light meditation is another way we can bring a sense of energetic protection into our day-to-day life, like a bubble, while connecting to our spirit within.

 As you sit in your home or favorite place to meditate, focus on the hum of the refrigerator or the gentle drip of a tap, or perhaps a heater, anything that is making a constant noise. In focusing on a consistent sound, and not unlike the three-minute breathing meditation, your mind will quiet. By connecting to an object outside of us, we can connect to the innermost quiet place within us. We are then connected to our highest expression of ourselves, and that vibration naturally brings matching energies into our day.

I've noticed that when I practice this, the day flows more smoothly. Cars on the road even seem to drive more calmly, too. It feels funny to write this because how could that be true? It's simply the new perspective that we gain when we complete a meditation like this, as we can now see the world from a place of space and grace and might even feel safer to be all of who we are. After meditation, we might agree that some shifts have taken place within, as subtle as they might be. Notice as you go on with your day if you feel these changes. Some folks say that they feel more patient with themselves and are more mindful when completing tasks.

Another meditation we can practice is to imagine a word that we'd like to feel in alignment with.

 For instance, perhaps you want to align with the word "clarity." You can think back to a time when you had a lot of clarity, when you knew exactly what to do, whom to call, and what to say, and in no time, you become the feeling of clarity. If you want to bring a sense of joy into your life, focus on the word "joy" by remembering activities you've done before that brought you joy, and feel it now within your heart.

We have everything within us to be the energy that we would like to receive. With this practice, we can even see someone else in a different light than what they are. If someone is feeling unwell or has an illness, we can call to mind the words "healthy," "happy," or "free." Sending them this beautiful energy is a way to bring more love and kindness into our world and into our own being. Don't just think of them being healthy, happy, or free—really feel into the energy. Feelings in our body trump any thoughts of what we would like to manifest. Try to invoke a feeling of something that you'd like the most, visualize what that is, and see it happening.

All of life is practice. The goal of practice is not to make you perfect, as the saying goes, but rather, to help you live a life of deeper awareness. All these prayers, rituals, and meditations help us to live lives of meaning, connection, and love in alignment with our four minds: our intellect, our bodily intelligence, our more expansive identities, and our connection with cosmic consciousness.

MEDITATING WITH AWARENESS

In the silence, we take nourishment from the deepest part of us. In the stilling of the mind and body through meditation, we can feel the world around us while still listening to the wisdom of the heart.

Meditation is not only sitting and finding quiet within, but also observing with great wonder what is happening and being felt in the everyday moments of our outer lives. In this way, all of life can be a meditation class. Meditation can be here and now because the quiet within is often just a breath away.

"Keep it simple," said the Dalai Lama. "There is no need for temples; no need for complicated philosophy. Our own brain, our own heart is our temple; our philosophy is kindness."

Meditation, or contemplation, is the seventh limb of yoga in Patanjali's *Yoga Sutras*. These eight limbs or steps act as guideposts for how we can live a more meaningful and purposeful life. They invite us to live a moral and ethical existence as we focus our attention on "healthy living" in all the many understandings of this phrase.

As you read on, please bring with you what yoga teacher Seane Corn calls "the god of your own heart," if at all. By this I mean that meditation or contemplation is not a replacement for any kind of faith that you have and that you know works for you. If you are a yoga person or teacher, you might remember learning about this limb of yoga in your teacher training. Learning about the sutras in their most basic form is quite simply a way of moral and ethical existence. Our learning overflows from there and leads to a lifetime of curiosity and understanding. Even after two decades as a yoga student and teacher, I still often refer to the sutras for guidance and, as Patanjali might say, to refine my personality—or gain more awareness in my body—and develop an energetic awareness of myself and all beings. This lays the foundation, preparing us to delve deeper into our senses and minds, and into embodying the higher vibrational state of consciousness that is available to not just a few, but to all of us.

Returning to ourselves doesn't always feel good, and I mean in the physical sense. To get in touch with and have a loving relationship with our body and what we are experiencing feels essential, but what if we have an injury that makes it uncomfortable to sit for long periods? When I first tried meditating, there was so much pain in my lower back that I chose not to continue and did *asana* practice instead. A major cause of lower back pain can sometimes be connected to simply sitting for prolonged times. There are other reasons like bulging disks or osteoarthritis. The more common thought is that the more we sit, the less we use our stabilizing muscles, causing them to weaken and struggle to do their job when we need them.

What is incredible about yoga asanas is that we strengthen and stretch our muscles in a balanced way and with the right sequence of poses. When we have weak or even tight muscles in the lower back and stomach area, we can get lower back pain from the simplest of actions. Learning to practice a few functional asanas that can mimic simple actions like getting in and out of the car can be super helpful for us. Take your time to explore your local yoga studios to find the best fit and teacher for you. Always remember to adapt your practice and asanas to how your body feels in each moment and be gentle with yourself as you listen closely to your body's cues.

Years into practicing, I realized that I was focusing too much on my body's flaws. Practicing meditation was just too difficult. As I was meditating during that time, and also during my younger years of life, I didn't really understand that I was not my body. I thought even the pretty face I was fortunate to be given was almost the only thing that was good about me. So, when things started to change in my body, as all bodies are wont to do, I felt that my worth was wrapped up in the way that I looked. When I only focused on the so-called flaws of my body, my self-esteem plummeted, and I began to speak negatively to myself. The way that we speak to ourselves and even the tone we do it in affects our self-worth too. Eventually, after realizing what I was doing to myself, I slowly began replacing my negative thoughts with positive ones. I reprogrammed the way I spoke to myself, ultimately helping me to ground my energy and to build a more authentic form of self-esteem. I also found that nourishing my body with things that are good for me was helpful too. Sometimes that means going to my favorite yoga class, eating some chocolate, or getting a massage. Other times it is a walk outside to remember that the world is a big place, bringing things into perspective as the energy of nature washes over me.

When I see my body, face, and life from a broader perspective, through a yoga practice, walking, or just simply taking some deep breaths, I remember that true freedom lies within. Today I feel far more comfortable in my own skin and love my body for the experience of being inside of it, and I'm not so focused on what it could be doing better for me. It isn't my servant, and it doesn't work for me. It is, and will always be, a good friend that supports me in my journey. The paradox is that we are and we are not our physical bodies. I like to say that our body is essentially on loan, and it will one day be given back to the earth. So, while we are here living in these bodies, may we feel the beauty of who we are while remembering that we are much more than any physical form.

Some days when I would be so hard on my body, I wouldn't practice at all. Other days I would try to push through the pain, and in the process, I'd only create more unease. I didn't understand that my body needed to be held in awareness—that I needed to embrace and accept my feelings, as they were, by seeing them honestly without trying to change them.

I began to learn the lesson that when I treat myself with patience and compassion and return to a beginner's mindset, my back pain lessens.

To bring awareness to the areas that need more breath, acceptance, and unconditional love feels important to our mental health. Every day is new, every yoga shape and moment new, and if we go into practice thinking that we know how it's going to go, then we lose the kind of innocence that our practice can bring us. Simply slowing down to feel the inner body and to be present to it in the moment is more than enough. The feeling of being present should resemble visiting an old friend, communing in a yoga pose, or folding the laundry mindfully.

In a nutshell, meditation is a process that results from a successful turning inward and a knowledge that there is a higher understanding more radiant than what our thinking mind and our intellect can provide.

With it, we usually understand that life, and our life, isn't only about our mental or primal way of being, but it is all-encompassing. In building a consistent meditation practice, we flow with the river of life and see that meditation is not just a moment in time where we sit and are separate from life, nor is it an escape or a rejection of life. Meditation has the potential to heal our broken parts. It can also help us to have a gentle distance from our feelings and activities, yet still be cognizant that they are there without feeding into them unnecessarily, to just be the observer of them.

Through meditation, we become more courageous and we can work through challenges more calmly while being centered in our bodies. If we need to solve a problem, we can sit and observe what's present without changing anything or finding a solution—we just witness it. During meditation, when we observe from our head to our heart, our mind becomes less busy and solutions can arise from a calmer, more balanced place.

I find that when my mind is left on its own to solve a problem, it begins to introduce complications based on old excuses and interpretations that are not my truth. Now, when I witness my mind, I hear my inner voice asking me whether I'm anchored in thoughts and images, in the body, or the space outside, and whether I've entered into a higher space where the ordinary mind can be witnessed.

Once we've experienced this space, we don't have to blindly accept a belief system or others' opinions, thoughts, and judgments. Meditation lets us see for ourselves what's true for us. When our thoughts and emotions vanish, when we are in direct contact with the actual nature of our mind, then no one's opinions, judgments, or views will sway us. But how do we maintain a practice like this? Me, I can forget so easily, but if I get up for a few minutes, several times a day, and move around enough to embody my body, everything feels okay in the world. Sometimes, by feeling the sun's rays on my face, sipping some tea very slowly, or petting my dog, I'll remember my practice again.

MEDITATION IS FOR ANYONE

Anyone can be a meditator right where our bodies are today. We don't need to eat better, stop smoking, or curb our anxiety to start; we simply need to come as we are. Bad habits or uncomfortable mental states can sometimes fall away as we add meditation into our daily routine. Just making time for meditation is like building a temple of love and acceptance in our hearts. If starting a meditation practice sounds absolutely not for you, you can begin by sitting or lying down and just be with the movement of your breath for 30 seconds and work your way from there, adding a little more time to every session. Whatever you end up doing, or not doing, the most important thing is to not be hard on yourself.

Practicing awareness or mindful meditation is different from formal sitting or lying down meditation. When we practice sitting meditation on a consistent basis, then practicing awareness meditation in our everyday lives becomes a natural byproduct, strengthening our overall awareness in all that we do and say. Cooking, folding laundry, and stacking the dishwasher are all great ways to practice mindful awareness throughout the day. Being mindful of each lift of our hand, each look of our gaze usually leads to peace and calm. When we forget about practicing, we can sometimes feel disconnected from ourselves, or our minds might go down the thinking mind rabbit hole more easily—the opposite of peace and calm. This can cause some of us to feel mild depression, often in the form of feeling a lack of our own importance, which is the opposite of what most of us are looking for in life.

Our monkey minds are often jumping from one thing to another when we're not practicing present-moment mindfulness. Sometimes our awareness is hijacked from the present by trips down fantasy lanes from the past, where we can sometimes edit our experiences and make things seem really good when, in fact, they were subpar at best. This might look like romanticizing a past relationship or an old job that really brought us a good deal of pain.

When we are not aware of our mind wandering, it can be tough to be here now. We don't need to give in to our minds jumping all over the place—we do have a say in where it goes, which is the point of mindfulness meditation. We can make good choices that strengthen our ability to concentrate on the present moment. What I try to do is to think about my past or plan for the future in small doses, such as scheduling my tasks in the morning, or allowing time for a reflective journaling session. Then, I am more likely to stay in the moment the rest of the day. Having a yoga practice is another way we can strengthen our connection to the present moment. Yoga, quite simply, supports us in being more mindful. As we follow our in-breath and out-breath while practicing, we are instantly brought back into our sensations and our body, mind, and heart connection. Our breath is a constant link to the path of presence. When our attention goes to it, there is no past or future, and things almost feel timeless.

REACTING VERSUS RESPONDING

Another way to practice mindful awareness is in situations that might be less comfortable. Perhaps this is in a meeting: observe yourself, pay attention to your reactions in your mind, but don't say them out loud. Perhaps you already do something like this? I do this a lot with my teenagers. As you might imagine, if I said everything that came into my head, and in a reactionary way, our relationship would suffer.

When I look at my children, not only do I do my best to accept them as they are, but I also remind myself that they are human beings in the making. They will and do already have their own opinions about things, and those won't always be aligned with mine. The same goes for my husband. If I said everything that came into my mind, it would be hard to live under the same roof with the respect that we enjoy today. I'm not recommending that we should stuff down and suppress any feelings that are bubbling up to the surface—it just means that whatever is coming up is not as important as the love and respect that we share. I'm also learning not to need to make someone else's opinion wrong (especially in my own head). When I have done this in the past, it only makes me feel like I'm right, and not much peace lives in being right. This can be really hard for me not to do, but perhaps it's more truthful to say that it's harder on my ego. And although our ego often works to keep us safe, it doesn't always serve us well in our close relationships.

Awareness meditation can also be practiced in moments when our inner child takes over. This "little one" inside of us likes to be seen, heard, and have its energy felt. If something happened to us when we were little, like not getting our needs met, that little one usually comes out in our adult relationships. Let's say that as a child, all you wanted was to be heard and seen by your parents. One day, they are in the middle of a conversation when you interrupt them. They get mad at you and call you a naughty boy or girl. Now, as an adult, you will need to do the work to repair that feeling of rejection, which came as a result of wanting to be heard and seen. Usually, our parents don't think their reaction was harmful or wrong, so how can we blame them? Not blaming or shaming them, and ourselves, is a key ingredient in finding and keeping the peace and not "acting out" similar scenarios in our big girl and big boy relationships as adults.

Usually, if we are triggered by being interrupted by someone and we are grown adults, it's probably safe to say that we don't even realize it's happening. And the other person is most likely our partner or one of our closest people whom we feel the safest being with. The other person may just pass it off and apologize for interrupting because let's be honest, that did happen. But what if the triggered person blows it out of proportion and embarrasses the other in front of friends? Let's start with the thought that no one is wrong or right. Then we can acknowledge that these kinds of reactions need compassion first and foremost. When we feel triggered, in an ideal world we will stop for a moment and "be the watcher" of our triggered reaction and go into the depth of the root cause of this pain, which could then serve us on the path to healing.

Alas, life isn't always that clean, and we tend to see others' shortcomings much more than we can see our own. But what if we stopped judging them and started to consider that their actions are coming from their own early childhood wounding, and really have little to nothing to do with us? Could it be that their inner child would like some validation around being seen in the conversation? Perhaps this is them re-enacting that moment with their parents when they were called "naughty" for interrupting, playing out in their adult life. If this is true, then by simply witnessing the trigger, we are taking the first step in understanding, loving, and accepting them just as they are with the conditioning that was handed down to them, be it unconsciously or consciously. Wouldn't we want them to treat us with that same compassion? In choosing to be compassionate with ourselves and with our everyday conversations with our loved ones, we can usually diffuse a situation before it becomes something bigger. At the end of the day, not only are we responsible for our own responses, but we are also responsible for our energy in the room. Not our friends' or our family members' behavior, just ours.

While I try to bring awareness meditation to all that I do, I often fall short. I have to remind myself that when others are not doing their part, I am the only person I have control over. And I know that the little one in me who sometimes had an out-of-control upbringing likes to make sure everyone is peaceful with each other. This is the part of me who learned to be a people pleaser, and who would do anything not to have anyone raise their voice. Feelings of unsafety and uncertainty can well up inside of me if I'm not pausing (inside) to see (witness), feel (with my body), and give myself self-compassion. If I don't remember these things, if I haven't had good sleep, or if I am feeling ill, all of this self-compassion stuff can honestly go out the window.

As a living and breathing human, I often make mistakes. It's as though a tantrum of sorts bursts out and the little one within me turns into an adult dragon ready to slay anyone in my path. After many decades of this and seeing the pain that it causes to myself and my loved ones, I have realized there really is another way, and it's self-compassion. Our past wounds can pop up in our present life without much, if any, notice at all, so when we practice mindful awareness in our everyday life, we can begin to see where we are getting reactive, and allow us to choose a more loving response.

I used to judge myself, feeling like something must be wrong with me when I would get reactive. But that was before I developed a self-compassionate relationship with myself. The truth is that our healing is quite circular, almost like an infinity sign. As we work through the pain we are feeling in the present moment, anchor that to our past wounds, and practice self-compassion, we have another opportunity for healing. We are often most reactive with the folks who are closest to us probably because we feel the safest with them to be ourselves. My little one didn't always get her needs met, nor did her voice seem to matter to those around her. So when uncomfortable situations arise and I'm feeling triggered, I remind myself that speaking up in a self-compassionate way in the safety of my close relationships is the best I can do to heal her. The home that I have created today feels safe—not perfect, but safe, which is the best that I could ask for. When I chose my life partner almost 15 years ago, I didn't know that it could be this way. In choosing him, a new path was created, and a new life.

When we witness ourselves with compassion and make our healing a priority, everyone around us benefits too. When we are mindfully aware, we are so much more conscious of our impact on our closest relationships. During any conflict with our beloveds, when we remember who we are, we don't feel the need to involve ourselves in power struggles. When we feel disconnected from ourselves and forget to be self-compassionate, our need for power over something or someone deepens, and that only serves to disconnect and separate us even more from ourselves and the other person, which is certainly not the outcome we want. Hurt people hurt other people, but when we make healing ourselves our priority, not only do we hurt other people far less, but we can become an instrument for their healing as well.

INTEGRATING SITTING MEDITATION WITH EVERYDAY MINDFULNESS

We can't always expect to run on the momentum of the goodness from our regular sitting meditation practice. It's wonderful to have a formal sitting practice and when we integrate that with everyday mindfulness, life feels more peaceful. Sitting meditation can be a good foundation, but I'm not convinced that we can rely on it alone to keep us feeling balanced and completely mindfully aware. What I know is that if I am practicing mindful awareness, then I don't always have to look to my sitting meditation practice to renew me. I can be more open and lose some of the expectations that I sometimes unconsciously place on my sitting practice.

It feels important now more than ever to develop a "state of being" not just on our cushion, but into our lives. How we interact with the world inside us is often a mirror of how we are on the outside. Meditation can help us grow and become more skillful at living lives of peace and happiness—but let's face it, it's not realistic to be calm and blissful all the time. We're going to get angry, we're going to get frustrated, we're going to get impatient, and we're going to get irritated. I'm advocating for not pushing these emotions away, but instead, witnessing them as they arise. When we get good at witnessing our emotions, we learn not to be consumed or confused by them—they just are what they are. They don't need to define us or make us who we are, but we can learn about ourselves through them. Essentially, we might look at our darker emotions as an energy passing through us, and not a fixed nor complete understanding of who we are. In other words, I don't see myself as an angry person—I see myself as a person experiencing anger, and this too will pass.

NATURE MEDITATION

Perhaps you already have a meditation practice that you like that helps connect you with the present moment. If you do, this might be a good time to do one of them or get up and take a gentle and mindful walk outside or around your home.

 It's sometimes easier to be in the present moment while walking in nature because there tend to be fewer distractions than at home or the workplace. Here are some questions I like to ask myself as I walk in nature:

- How can I be in touch with the present moment?
- What smells are present?
- What sounds am I hearing?

We don't need to get caught up in thinking about specific answers, such as the types of birds we're hearing, but simply be the "listening," if you will, as though it's an orchestra of sound penetrating us — we can hear, feel, and experience the sound through our whole body.

As we walk, with each step we begin to ground into our beingness, approaching each moment with awareness—smelling the air around us, taking in all the sights, and feeling grateful for simply being alive. Remember, there is no expectation or pressure that you'll stay out of your head and in your body— just do your best. Being present-minded helps us to feel grounded in our bodies. This isn't just something to do when life isn't going so well—this can truly become our way of life. It can support us right where we are and with any pain that we might be feeling. When we are totally present, we're not adding to our pain by going into stories of the past or worrying about the future. We are simply present with "what is."

If we are employed, our work or office environment can often feel like a harder place to practice mindful awareness because there's often pressure to be productive and get things done quicker and in less time. So what I'm going to suggest might sound counter-intuitive. What if we actually allow ourselves more time to do a task? In slowing down, we can focus on one thing at a time while continuing to grow our mindful focus at our job. Unfortunately, notifications, messages, and alerts are often geared to bring us into either our past or future, so taking at least a little rest from our computer or phone can help support us in being in the moment. Perhaps this looks like turning our phone on Do Not Disturb, or placing the phone in another room while we focus on a task.

Meditation is a wonderful practice to have to bring us to present moment awareness while bringing along a mindful energy into our daily lives. Over time, and with practice, notice how you begin to evolve.

MEDITATION AND WOUNDS

Wounds are a part of our lives. Whether we were abandoned at birth, didn't receive what we needed as a child, a parent died when we were young, or we grew up too quickly caring for an unwell family member, we have all experienced trauma to greater or lesser degrees. Sitting in meditation can be a wonderful way to witness our wounds rising to the surface. Not only our own personal wounds, but our collective wounds—so many of us are sensitive to the violence, political strife, environmental destruction, and other ways that we wound each other and our planet.

Through my own experience of staying present with my wounds, I have come to the conclusion that if I am *feeling* my wounds, then I am *not* my wounds. My wounds are present, but they are not me; they are passing through me, but they do not define or make me who I am.

Recently, I felt triggered by the lack of love in the collective field, and during my meditation, a flood of tears came rushing down my cheeks. This was around 10:00 in the morning and my children were already at school and my husband was working from home. I've had these feelings come up before, so I knew to be gentle with myself as I went to sit in a quiet area in the sun just outside of my home to understand where and what the root cause was for my feeling this way. It was a time in the world when our leaders were fighting with each other. Trump was our president and there was, to say the least, a lot of drama, back-and-forth name-calling, and other uncomfortable goings on. I guess I took them to heart in a way. And just to be clear, I'm not going to discuss a particular political side, because as I look back, it isn't about that. Because of what was happening in our collective and in "real time," I felt transported back, through feeling and emotion, to a time when everyone in my family was fighting and getting upset with each other. A time in my life where I didn't feel supported and where I blamed myself for my mum and dad divorcing and hating one another.

These times occurred throughout my childhood at different moments, but especially when I was three years old. I recall one particular moment of feeling betrayed and left alone to fend for myself. I wrote a lot of these stories in my teaching memoir, *A Life Worth Living: A Journey of Self-Discovery, Mindfulness, Yoga, and Living in Awareness*. Even as a 45-year-old woman with a family of my own and a good marriage, these feelings began to resurface. My lower back even started to hurt again as it always did when I was little, and I felt this kind of pressure in my body and a rise of emotions. I knew that my body was letting me know there was more healing to be done.

I began to take a trip down memory lane and visit these places within me that, for whatever reason, needed more time to heal. I ended up canceling my plans for the day to take some time to be with my own awareness. I went to a place where it was easy for me to connect to my true nature: our local reservoir. Being in nature has a way of soothing my aching heart and allowing me to name what I think is happening. It was the medicine that I needed in that moment to feel whole again. It might have been easier to stuff my feelings down for another day, but I know that when I've done that before, it never works in the long run. I usually end up blowing something totally unrelated out of proportion, and in turn, hurting myself and those that I love around me. This time, I knew I needed to soothe the little one in me. I needed to be with her and let her know that she is loved no matter what chaos is happening in the collective, and all of which I have no control over. I needed to nurture myself and be with my beloved dog, Rosie, around the water—I needed to stay there until I felt the strength to be out in my life again with the people who love me so much. It has taken me years, decades really, to take care of myself like this. But however long it takes doesn't matter—for in the end, once we realize that it's our own love, acceptance, connection, and validation of ourselves that we need, there is no turning back.

I knew I had touched a place deep within that needed more healing. I felt the energy of all of us as individuals, with our bad decisions on display, and how we were feeling less than love for ourselves. When our wounds rise to the surface during our day or in meditation, how do we find the courage and comfort to sit with them while not pushing them away? That day, I knew that if I could just slow things down enough, I might have a chance to love myself and accept that, like everything in life, it would pass—but not until the emotion moved through me and shared its insight and healing.

Here are five tips that have helped me when I'm experiencing deep wounding.

Get really clear that something has been triggered inside but know that you're going to be okay. If possible, wipe your schedule clean for at least a few hours. This is a huge opportunity to harness great love for yourself, and it starts by creating space around what's happening.

Accept what you're going through. Be honest with yourself. Whether you are experiencing a lot of tears or not, this is not the moment to put yourself last, or even second. Healing is something that, if we catch it in the moment, can have everlasting effects on our self-worth. Essentially, we are becoming the kindness we wish to see in the world. Whatever it takes, do it! Get the kids to a playdate, tell your supervisor at work you have a medical issue that you are dealing with (it's true). Say what you need to say to put yourself at the top of the list. Let your kids, partner, or roommates know that you are going through something and that it's not about them. Be vulnerable and speak from your heart. Let the ones closest to you know that you just need some time to be. It can make all the difference.

Be gentle with the process. In the end, the only thing you may feel you did was create space in your schedule. Put your attention and faith in the journey, not the destination. Congratulate yourself on taking care of yourself. In the midst of the storm, remember to keep calm and take refuge in love and the practices that support your heart—physically, mentally, emotionally, and spiritually.

Drop into your heart and do what you know brings you closer to your true nature. Maybe that's being outside near the ocean, or walking in your backyard or neighborhood or city. For some, it may be listening to a favorite podcast that brings a calming feeling to your being. Become gentle and quiet so you can remember who you are in the midst of it all. This will ensure a deep level of self-care. This does not mean your mind will automatically become quiet, but if you can sit or lie down in a quiet space to witness your thoughts, it will encourage your mind to become quieter. Something happens when we sit in contemplation or meditation. With the body still, the mind might still be busy with thoughts, but it also allows it to notice that it is not the only important part of the body. Our mind is important, but so are our kidneys, our liver, our backs, and all the parts of our body that constantly work in the background to bring us to balance and well-being.

Try not to over-analyze what's happening. If possible, find an activity that drops you into your heart space. That way, you can be your own best teacher, guide, and therapist. It's simply about becoming gentler with yourself, accepting, and trusting the process. Don't judge or be hard on yourself. As you see these visitors rise into your mind's eye, say hello to them and acknowledge their presence without giving them a chair to sit in your heart. No matter what you are going through, staying present with difficult emotions and thoughts will ultimately increase your capacity to love and listen, and be your own best friend.

After you've taken these steps, getting outside help might be next on your list. Perhaps it's a massage, spiritual counseling, therapy, or a meditation workshop with a focus on compassion. In the end, no amount of outside help can love and care for us the way we can for ourselves. Yet having supportive folks in our lives and community feels essential for our overall well-being.

WATER MEDITATION

Thanks to the formless, flowing and almighty state of water, it has long been helpful to support us with any mental and physical traumas. It also supports us in feeling more ease and calm. It can relieve stress and anxiety, boost our energy, and give us more resiliency throughout the day. Whether you choose to meditate in or near water, the power of water meditation is profound.

 If you are lucky enough to live close to a body of water like a beach, pond, or river, perhaps take regular visits and feel it out for yourself. Clearing your energy and mind can be as simple as placing your attention on the waves or ripples in the water while relaxing your body, and if your mind seems to wander off and you notice it, simply bring it back to the movements of the water.

Another water meditation involves drinking water. After you have read this section, please go ahead and get yourself a glass of water, close your eyes, then ask your higher self, God, universe, guides, or the archangels to infuse their love and energy into the water so that it can act as medicine and a refuge for the self. When you drink it, notice the loving energy that you and your spirit guides have placed into it. May you feel the cleansing and healing effects from the inside/out. Now light a candle, and if you have an intention for the day, say it now (three times). Your intention could be anything that is in your heart and rises to your awareness in the moment. It can be something like, *may it be a peaceful day, may I experience a day of clarity, may I move through my day with deep awareness,* or *may I feel safe and loved.* Then take a sip of your water with your mindful intention.

Practicing things like water meditation is like making deposits of love into our energetic bank account. This sacred, gentle, and simple meditation can have a huge impact on how we feel, especially in turbulent times. By getting up in the morning, saying a few prayers, lighting a candle, and perhaps doing the same before going to sleep, we feel more connected to ourselves. This kind of helpful ritual brings us to the gates of heaven inside our own hearts. I like to say that when we do this, we reboot ourselves for the next moment. The next moment will be what the past moment (energy) was, and this sets the tone for all the moments going forward. Once we make the time to tune in to ourselves, gratitude for the life we are living is possible. Through this realization, we anchor into our heart center.

CULTIVATING PEACE WITH AWARENESS

Meditation doesn't answer all our questions, but it creates space around our inquiries, allowing us to be present when "answers" present themselves.

Did you know that it is not just okay for us to have an inner life that is peaceful during times of great struggle, but essential? And that we need not always fall victim to our empathetic reactions? The very thing that is our superpower can also be something that hurts us more than anything else. Empathy allows us to be compassionate and caring for ourselves and others, but it can also lead us to feel immobilized.

Has this ever happened to you? Or has it been coming up for you lately? You wouldn't be alone if it has. Between living through a pandemic, and as I write this, Putin's war with Ukraine, it's easy to feel that the outer world seems too much to handle. And it's certainly not about feeling guilty about it, or being hard on ourselves when this happens either. For those of us who identify as being highly sensitive, we can sometimes struggle with the energy that comes at us from the world, especially if it's turbulent. One of the best things we can do—for ourselves, our friends, and the world—is to be as peaceful as possible. We can have a practice centered around peace.

If you are a yoga practitioner, you know that we also live our lives off the mat as well as on it. But if you are also, like me, a parent with a household and responsibilities to manage, inviting internal peace into your life doesn't always go as planned. If this sounds familiar, I offer some tips for inviting peace off of the mat and into your home, your work, and your life.

COMMIT TO GENTLE MORNINGS

Time for reflection is the much-needed medicine for processing life's constant changes. Never underestimate the power of sipping your coffee mindfully before opening your phone. Upon waking, set your intentions for the day. What would you like to align yourself with? Though life sometimes has other plans for us, it's generally true that what you focus on and give energy to will come into being.

MENTAL HEALTH DAY IS EVERY DAY

Whenever you notice your mental health declining, do one small thing that brings you calmness. Maybe it's in the ritual of making and sipping a cup of tea. Or maybe it's in practicing a few restorative poses while feeling the sun's rays coming through the window. One small movement toward slowing down and being mindful can make a huge difference in moving to a place of peace! In these few moments of inner connection, we feel spacious and remember who we are.

LET GO

Toward the end of the day, make some time to sit, closing your eyes and watching your breath. It doesn't need to be a long time, maybe just a minute if that's all you have. Once you realize that you are holding onto something—be it something that someone said, or a deeper wound—letting go becomes possible. That's why a little afternoon reflection yoga time might even become your new favorite thing. You'll just feel lighter, and who doesn't want to feel that?

EMBRACE THE UNKNOWNS OF LIFE

In the end, what we don't know can't hurt us—it's only the "knowns" in life that tend to haunt us. If you don't know, just carry on! Sit in the unknown of "not knowing." It's not always comfortable, but it's a very good space for us to be in. When I find myself uncomfortable with all the unknowns in life, I find ways to invite more space into my life . . . inviting more of my "human-beingness" (spirit) energy, or heart center, rather than simply defaulting to the thinking mind all the time. Embrace the unknowns, and trust that you are "becoming." Our life's journey is transformation, so be patient. Remember: we don't always need to be achieving something. Being present with evolution is more than enough.

DREAM, MOVE, AND BREATHE

We must allow space in our life to dream! If we don't allow ourselves to dream, life can get pretty mundane. The "being" part of us human beings loves to dream, loves to dance, and loves to spend time in nature. Create more ways to feel joyful. Is it by coloring, singing, or getting outside? Don't wait for life to become overwhelming to invite the element of dreaming into your being. Life is amazing—we just need to focus on the beauty that's already there.

Don't forget to move your body, sweat, and get the toxins out. Just do your yoga if it's the only activity that you like; otherwise, you probably won't be consistent with it. Something happens to us when we make time to move our body: the happy endorphins start to flow and the heaviness of the world begins to melt away. Breathe deeply, just one conscious breath in and one conscious breath out. This could be all you need to interrupt an anxious thought pattern. Never underestimate the power of the breath!

TURN OFF MEDIA AND SCREENS

This is pretty obvious stuff, although it's so hard to do sometimes! It has become such a habit for most of us to scroll through messages, social media, or the news. When unpleasant news or messages flood into our awareness, they can nullify all the peace we have brought into our day. Be mindful of what and how much you allow into your heart's home. At our home, we have "No Screen Sundays." At first, it was hard to get our teens on board (and some Sundays are still a challenge!), but it's totally worth it. We are so much better for it, and in the end, we have more fun as a family. Alternative activities for us are playing a card game together, cooking, baking, and going for a family walk in the neighborhood.

CULTIVATE A GRATEFUL HEART

This is also easy to say, but how do we make gratitude a practice? For me, it might be one or two sentences that I say out loud to myself as I get into bed at night. *Thank you for my day, thank you for keeping me safe, thank you for the clean water and food that I was fortunate to eat today.* Or if there is something you're going through or working on, send a few thoughtful words out to the universe, and watch how quickly grace enters into your awareness. Sometimes I'll say something like this: *Dear Universe: I give you permission to work on X, Y, Z (life situations), and when I wake, I hope you'll provide me with clarity and direction.* When I remember to do this, I almost always understand what I need to do.

Sometimes we just might need to stop looking for the miracles, and simply be the miracle.

BEING PRAYERFUL WITH AWARENESS

Pay some attention to your inner body for a moment. It's hard to slow down and be mindful when everything is moving so fast.

Prayer is an essential part of bringing peace into our lives. But it can be hard—not because it requires intellect or knowledge or a big vocabulary, but because it requires humility and self-compassion. The need for prayer can sometimes come from a profound sense of one's brokenness, or from a need that is asking to be met. Sometimes, it can quite simply be the need to get out of trouble quickly—a feeling of, *please God, I'll do anything!* To be connected to something bigger than oneself, to have a deeper knowing of the connection between all of us, and to acknowledge this through a consistent practice of prayer, creates a bridge from the physical plane to the spirit body.

Living more *prayerfully* also assists us in being more aware. And it doesn't necessarily mean that we have to belong to any religion. Being prayerful means believing in the highest part of who we are: the conscious energy that lives behind our personality, and the part that connects us with each other.

WHAT MIGHT ARISE DURING PRAYER

Being prayerful can help us to feel less alone in our life. We feel more connected to ourselves, to others, and have a deeper sense of meaning that fills up our hearts. I know that when I close my eyes to pray, there is a depth that I feel about me. It feels as though I have entered into the unknown and can access parts of me that I never knew, or sometimes forget, exist. Learning to pray is about developing a deeper relationship with ourselves and with the god that speaks to you and your faith. These moments in prayer bond us to a greater, yet more available energy that is not separate from the right here and nowness of our lives. When we pray, we are not praying away to some high-up place in the sky, somewhere away from our lives or what we are experiencing here on earth. We are grounded in all that's happening in our human lives while remaining connected to our more expansive selves that operate at a higher resonance, if you will. You will know that you have entered into this space because a sense of comfort may overcome you. It might feel almost like you've returned from a very long trip, and you finally step into your home and smell all the comforts and feel the calming energy that coming home can bring.

Communicating with our higher self is like communing with the most conscious part of who we are, and we can take refuge in and rely upon prayer whenever we need to access that higher self. Our awareness deepens too as the act of saying a spontaneous prayer can function like a kind of internal journaling. We lay our intentions out to the universe and become clearer about what we would like. We often feel a higher vibration inside ourselves, and that can help us to attract the same energy in our outer lives. While we are in prayer, we might ask ourselves what we would like to align with. Is it love, inner peace, or a sense of contentment? Maybe all three? The answer may not and does not need to appear right away, so just be with the quietude as you open yourself to a spacious awareness, the foundation on which answers can arrive.

Sitting with our eyes closed and in prayer, we have the opportunity to go into the depth of our being but also into different areas of our body or life that might need our attention. An injured elbow or a sensitive stomach may need our attention, or an emotion or difficult thought could come forth. When observing our inner emotional life, try to remember that although our thoughts often roll in unannounced or even unwelcome, we don't need to always believe them. Kind of funny, right? Perhaps we could consider them as waves of energy proceeding through the mind's screen. We don't necessarily need to give them our sustained attention if we don't want to—rather, we can just acknowledge them.

For example, I have this story rolling around in my head from time to time that the important women in my life always end up betraying me. This, of course, is not completely true (if at all). I believe it stems from not having a healthy attachment to my mother and father as a baby. I've read that our attachment style is shaped and developed in early childhood by our relationships with our parents. According to attachment theory, first developed by psychologist Mary Ainsworth and psychiatrist John Bowlby in the 1950s, we mirror the dynamics we had with our parents—or primary caregivers—as infants and children.

In reading about the various attachment types, I realized that I have an anxious attachment type. This, unfortunately, can lead to a sense of unworthiness that has me constantly striving for acceptance, approval, and validation from others. Yet at the same time other folks in my mind are considered good, worthy, and positive (just not me).

It's sad, really, but what might be even more sad and immobilizing is if I were unaware of this. When I remember that this is my attachment style and not the truth about who I am, I feel so much better. Instead of acting out (consciously or unconsciously) and trying to get attention because I feel unworthy, I can be compassionate with myself and own my feelings. It's quite discouraging when this story arrives yet again, but it doesn't need to get the best of me either. I see it as just one of my core wounds that I know needs constant attention. When I remind myself that it's the "little one" inside of me, who for whatever reason feels afraid and alone in the moment, I can approach the story and my little one with compassion.

I've come to see us as creators and co-creators of our life, but when we get stuck in our habitual stories, we box ourselves in and feel small, unseen, and to be honest, we're probably not in the very tangible here and now. But when we are honest with ourselves and compassionately recognize that our stories and wounds usually rise to the surface for our deeper healing, we take our power back.

Our stories and wounds are almost like a recurring dream or a record that keeps playing the same song over and over again, even when we're ready to move on. Remember that the little one in us is just trying to remain safe, so in loving her and letting her know that we see her, whether she's crying or behaving immaturely, we give ourselves the medicine we need to bring ourselves back to the nowness of our life. We can feel and see her cry out for attention, assure her that everything is okay, while not rushing her to get over it. We can help heal the wounded one within by offering her patient witnessing.

We can hold her for whatever amount of time she (or he or they) might need, and in doing so, allow her to release the painful negative energy of whatever story she's (re)living in the moment.

Sometimes in these moments, we might just need to stop everything we're doing and focus instead on comfort care. We can snuggle up under a blanket on the couch and watch television to nurture ourselves. We can take a warm, fragrant bath. We can invite our dog onto our bed and take a cat nap! We can light a candle and say a prayer for our little one's healing.

If you are like me and have an abandonment wound, this kind of self-care with self-acceptance when inner stuff comes up might feel foreign to you. But, if possible, work through these feelings anyway. They are like a muscle that just needs time and awareness to become stronger and more flexible too. We are totally worth it and, indeed, we matter. When we give ourselves permission to come as we are, everyone around us benefits too. There isn't a one-way street to freedom and liberation—our self-care encourages others to care for themselves as well. At the same time, when we remember who we are beyond our stories, we grow, heal, and take refuge in the company of ourselves. The healing comes, not because we need to fix something about ourselves, but because we are already whole. It comes because we remember the goodness of us to the very core of our being.

In the constant bombardment of our thoughts and emotions, may we be discerning and recognize when our little one just needs some time to be with us, without overanalyzing her.

PRAYING FOR OTHERS

Have you noticed that out of nowhere a family member, friend, or acquaintance can just pop into our minds? It's almost as though an image or a feeling of them appears right there in the forefront of our mind's screen. When they do, it can be an indication to send them a little sentence of your felt prayer. Tuck them into your heart and send them a ray of your light for continued healing, whatever their circumstances. Or on the other hand, they might be thinking of you, which is why they popped up in your mind—you might want to offer a prayer of gratitude for their attention.

What if folks who have in the past or who currently are treating us badly come into our awareness when we pray? There is no "correct" way to pray for them, but I have two suggestions. Perhaps you have a gut feeling in your body that you should pray for them, for their peace or their healing or their enlightenment. If it feels right and resonant, send them your prayer blessings. Forgiving ourselves and others is a powerful way to free up more space in our body and mind, helping us remember that we didn't just come from love, that we are love. The thing is, we don't have to agree, like, or appreciate what another person has done to us, or might be doing to us in real-time. Whatever's happened in our past or is happening in our present, we can wish them well-being and extend love anyway.

If you are not "there" yet, please be mindful to take it easy on yourself. We can't, and shouldn't, rush forgiveness when we don't feel it in our hearts and bodies. If someone comes into our prayers and their presence feels intrusive, it's okay to send them on their way. If I feel the unwelcome presence of someone or a spirit and I am in the middle of my prayers, I'll ask them to please go back to the light with compassion and love, especially if I feel I'm needing to protect my own space and energy field. If thoughts about someone create a heavy feeling or pain in my body during my prayers, I release those thoughts, and when I remember to do this, I always feel better in my body.

PRAYER AND HEALING

Unresolved pain and grief can get stored and stuck in the body if we don't discharge it. Receiving regular massages, acupuncture, nature walks, gentle yoga, water meditation, mindfulness practices, and yoga nidra are all ways that can support us in letting go of unresolved grief, tension, or pain. When there is built-up energy in my body, I'll take a walk outside, get the anger out into a pillow, or move my body with a few yoga shape positions. When I couple that with prayer, I'm able to shift the energy in my body and mind.

One of my favorite authors in the field of trauma and addiction is Dr. Gabor Maté, a Hungarian-Canadian physician who believes in the connection between mind and body health. Recently, he wrote the book *The Myth of Normal*, which quickly became a *New York Times* bestseller. He has a background in family practice and a special interest in childhood development, trauma, and potential lifelong impacts on physical and mental health including autoimmune diseases, cancer, attention deficit hyperactivity disorder (ADHD), addictions, and a wide range of other conditions. When I was listening to him on a podcast, he mentioned that working with a therapist trained in EMDR (eye movement desensitization and reprocessing) can be helpful in healing trauma.

He also says: "Trauma is not the bad things that happen to you but what happens inside you as a result of what happens to you." And: "Trauma is a fundamental disconnection from self." These two powerful quotes have helped me realize that no matter what others might think or say about my healing, it is only me who gets to decide what I need. It is only me who has processed (or is still processing) what has happened to me that has brought me to where I am today. My inner landscape and what I felt when I experienced repeated stress, abuse, and neglect as a child at the hands of young parents struggling with mental health and substance abuse issues had real, tangible effects on me. To be honest, it just isn't something that suddenly goes away, or we just get over. So far, I've spent most of my adult life working on myself to experience relief from PTSD, anxiety, and depression through yoga, therapy, acceptance, mindfulness, and other tools that support me in living fully and healthy. And yes, prayer, the subject of this chapter is one powerful tool as well.

There are many doctors, therapies, and healing modalities to explore, and there is certainly not a one-size-fits-all approach as we explore what might work well for us. Along with prayer, exploring things like yoga, tai chi, meditation, and any kind of somatic healing of the body are only just a few modalities available to support us in our healing journey. It could even be that nurturing ourselves, even only a little every day, can become our new normal.

TIPS FOR A PRAYER PRACTICE

When I enter into my prayer practice and no one is around, I find it helpful to speak my prayers out loud. It helps me to verbalize my thoughts, wishes, and needs. When I pray, I usually thank my highest self for chiming in with a few intuitive messages that came my way. If you are open to receiving, you'll be amazed at what your higher self may offer you. It does take getting quiet on a regular basis, and for many, the morning is best as we are more rested with less busy thoughts running through us. When we practice becoming quieter, intuitive messages have a better chance of coming to us and from our innermost well of healing. These messages are different from the usual thoughts of, say, your schedule coming into your mind. The messages that come from the soul usually come simultaneously with an actual feeling of *knowing* in your body.

If during prayer, your higher self sends you a message or a suggestion that you aren't ready to act on (you'll know this in your body), don't worry—you don't have to do anything you're not ready for. When this has happened to me, I've noticed that I'll usually manifest another similar situation later down the road and will have another chance to act on my higher self's wisdom. I've also noticed that my life is a lot easier when I trust myself and my own timing, and I remember that at my core lives love and goodness, and there is nothing untrustworthy there. By deeply listening inside, we feel, hear, and see our heart's voice and our body's mind as guidance. These are the inner communications coming from the universe, from which we are not separate. It's all waiting for us in the precious here and now.

Sometimes the guidance we receive in prayer may be something seemingly inconsequential like, *clear up your desk*. That directive might feel odd, but if we do clean it up, we might realize we are now open to new energy to finish that book we're writing or to sign up for that new course we've always wanted to take. Sometimes the guidance we receive may be far more profound, surprising even. This happened to me once, when I was considering which publisher I should reach out to for my first book. I lay down after a few yoga moves and prayerfully asked for guidance. As I listened to my question, the name Jennifer came to me, and the city she lived in. To be clear, I was already considering her among other publishers, but it was her name that I heard in that moment, and in the end, her company Mandorla Books was indeed the one who successfully published my first book (and this one too!). I found so much satisfaction in working on that book with her, and I felt more empowered because I didn't just hear the message that came in, but I listened to it fully and followed up on its guidance.

So listen to that quiet inner voice, even if the message or image that you receive may not make sense to you right away. These messages come from the highest place of who we are, from our soul, so just be as open as you can without any judgment. We are essentially a beautiful channel of life that is worthy of receiving good things. Getting into a harmonious relationship with our life is sometimes just reminding ourselves that we are beautiful. That we all consist of inner and outer beauty. May we remind ourselves that we are each on our own individual path and that we are exactly where we are supposed to be, and if there's somewhere else we need to go, our higher selves will inform us when we become quiet enough to hear that sometimes still voice within. Prayer opens our hearts and helps us become more aware of that wisdom-voice. It also allows us to feel so much more connected to who we really are, and the gifts we've come here to offer our beautiful world.

SOME PRAYERFUL ADVICE WHEN GOING THROUGH HARD TIMES

It helps to have someone in our lives with whom we can talk, whether it's a counselor or therapist, neighbor, best friend, or partner. It's so important to have folks we can rely on, the kind who can hold our hearts in life, and who will really listen to us, who we know won't shy away from us when life gets tough. Someone who treats us with dignity, non-judgment, and care. Having genuine people who care and want to see us thrive in the seasons of life fills up our hearts with all the good feels.

Having a spiritual practice is good, and especially if it involves a community or social activity. Otherwise, we might feel quite isolated in our healing. We are so much better together; we don't always need to do hard things on our own.

It's also good to remember that **we might need to change our paradigm** around prayer. When we pray, we don't have to think about some "God person" up in the sky. Think of prayer as more of a communion with the same light that lives in you, that lives in me, and all things. Of course, if you already have your own faith and certain beliefs, then be with them as you pray.

Keep in mind that prayer is not a petition for something, it's more of an asking for guidance. And things don't always have to be worked out on the spot. Remember that if you don't have any answer for something in the moment, that *is* often the answer in the moment—no answer at all! That answer may come tomorrow in your prayer time, or in some seemingly random email or text or voice you overhear in the market. Making yourself a channel for guidance doesn't mean that guidance will immediately come to you. Say thank you, even if you hear nothing in the moment, but keep your ears open.

Sometimes we don't know the answer we need, so our prayers can look something like, "I don't know what to do, I'm hurting, so please help me to see what is the best path for me." Or, "Dear higher self, help me to re-orientate my compass, because I don't know which way to turn or even which questions I should be asking." The times that I remember to do this, I am letting go of the outcome. And it is truly amazing how often the answers actually do come. It may come in that little voice within, from folks around me, in dreams, or in omens. Prayer is just about calling in the cooperative intelligence of the universe. That way, we don't feel alone or isolated, and we know we have a whole universe not just on our side, but that we are essentially our own mini-universe too.

In this way, we trust prayer by giving it time and space, and by not being urgent about needing an answer to it. Letting go of control may also require a certain amount of faith and fortitude to carry on without certainty, at least for now.

Having both a meditation and prayerful practice are some ways we can become more aware of our field of energy. Sometimes, it is hard to tell what is going on in our energetic field—we may feel a disturbance in our field, and not know entirely why. To strengthen the muscle of discernment, take a few minutes out of the day and just sit or lay down. If there are projects, people, or things coming to your mind, that is usually a sign of what's in our energy field. Take a minute or more to see those things in your mind's eye and gently allow them to move from your head down to your feet and into the ground where they can be held by the earth below us.

This process gives us a feeling of lightness, ease, and sovereignty. Once I ground whatever is in my energy field, I will call any energy back to me that I may have lost. It is easy to do: visualize a beautiful bright star above your head, and your energy being drawn back into it from all over the country, and sometimes, the planet. Once your energy is back in your star, imagine that light being poured down from the crown through each energy center (chakra) and down to your feet. This little meditation doesn't take that long, and I find it to be one of the best meditations for letting go of what's making me heavy, and returning to a state of light.

Getting up in the morning, lighting a candle, and saying some affirmations, prayers, and mantras are all ways we can bring harmony to our field of energy. This kind of loving attention and discipline brings us to the gates of heaven within our own hearts. We are essentially responsible for our energetic field and cutting the weeds that clog and clutter it. All it takes is a little practice and time. A shower meditation, a few stretches, or a walk might be all that is needed to "feel" fully and let go of what is no longer serving us. I learned something similar to this through the practices of an organization in Berkeley, California called "Intuitive Way" (https://intuitiveway.com/) and highly recommend studying with them—it was a game-changer for me in learning more about letting go (in an energetic sense).

PRAYER AT OUR WORKPLACES

Our workplaces can sometimes be stressful environments, so it's important to take moments to pause and bring mindful awareness there. Prayer isn't only for the home; we can also bring it to the workplace. We can ask for support from the invisible world or from within before going into a meeting, preparing an important document, or seeing a client. Here's an example prayer:

Dear higher self, guides, archangels, and those who have gone before me who are watching over me, I ask for your assistance with X [whatever it is you have upcoming, or if it's a person you're meeting, say their name] so that I may receive your light and energy and not feel exhausted by the task at hand or by the end of the day. My intuitive side, along with my scientific intellectual side, is supported by a divine energy that can be thought of as one mind.

You can say anything that comes naturally to you. Remember that you're your own best prayer maker. So if there are words that you would prefer to say, allow for your heart to speak them.

SUGGESTED PRAYERFUL RITUALS

When we ask for support through prayer and intention, we are merely connecting with what is already there. Our spirit support system is right there, waiting for us to ask for assistance, for they won't interfere without our asking. They also appreciate our grateful acknowledgment, so after your conference, meeting, phone call, or appointment, finish by thanking your guides and archangels and your wisdom body for the support you received, even if it doesn't feel like you received much in the moment. Everything is coming to us if we can just hold on to our faith and trust that we're on the correct path.

When your day is done, either sage your body fully — which involves burning sacred herbs to cleanse yourself or a space — or take a shower to cleanse any energy that needs to go back to the light with compassion. Ask your higher self, guides, and archangels to allow any energy that is not you to be sent to the light, and to send it there with compassion and love. If you see yourself as a highly sensitive or empathic type, you may experience more lightness by doing this, as you clean the energy field around and within you.

Make the closure of your work day easy, make it light—it needn't take more than 1-2 minutes. You could also sit in quiet meditation to check in with your body and experience what happened to you during the day, and what's happening now, as you prepare with intention to leave your day behind. Express your gratitude for all the good things that came your way today. Try and let go of the things that didn't go as well as you wanted them to go. We are only human, and we can only do our best, and that's it.

One more thing—make your office if you can, and most definitely your home, a place of beauty. Cut flowers from your garden or pick some up from the florist and place them in your cubicle or on your desk in your home office, and definitely in your home, especially where you can see them as you get off of work. The act of doing this is an act of meditation. Do this quietly and with a mindful, meditative energy. Maybe have some calming music on at the same time.

METTA (LOVINGKINDNESS) PRAYERS

If these morning and evening prayerful invocations speak to you, read them out loud to yourself and feel how they sit in your body once you're finished.

Morning Metta Invocation

*As a new day dawns, may I have the capacity to love
beyond the limitations created by fear
I am open to receiving assistance and guidance
Being present is my place of power
I offer my gratitude for the measure of health I have been given
May I be emotionally available for those who depend on me
May I be in a field of grace with everyone I encounter today
May I have faith and above anything else listen to my inner voice
My soul is full of warmth, wisdom, and love
I am safe,*

empowered,
and protected.

Evening Metta Invocation

Thank you for giving me another day
As I sleep, may all that does not serve me fall away easily
and effortlessly
I am grateful for my family and friends
I offer my sincere appreciation for my community
I offer my gratitude for the life I have been given and
With the deepest gratitude I remember the care and labor of those who
came before me, and who are watching over me now
As I rest, I ask for more clarity and guidance with X [an area of my life]
And when I wake, may I know what to do and feel rested enough to go
out and into the world with an open heart.

CREATING A SPACE FOR PRAYER: MAKING YOUR AL-TAR

Prayer can obviously be done anytime from anywhere, but people who have an altar in their home, a sacred space for meditation and prayer, find this place a powerful energy source. If you don't already have an altar, find a place in your home that can be reserved as your sacred place, be it a corner in your living room or office, and if you can, make it a room or corner that is yours alone. This is the special physical space that you can go to on a regular basis that reminds you of who you are, a beautiful embodied soul. Here you can light your candles, incense, and offer your prayers. I personally like to think of this area as a place of refuge, almost like a feeling of a lighthouse where I know I can go when I'm feeling disturbed, sad, or angry—or on the flip side, grateful, powerful, and filled with light and love. Some folks sit in meditation right in front of their altars in the morning, during the day, or before bedtime if they feel they need to or would like to. Practicing yoga or any kind of somatic movement in front of the altar is also another great way to remember what is most important to you as you move through your body.

In your sacred place, gather things that are of significance to you, things that you cherish. Perhaps a photo of your family, a Hindu deity, Jesus, Buddha, a sacred rock or crystal, divination cards, a bird feather, or a beautiful card your child made you. Another photo on the altar could be a photo of you at a younger age. When I've gone through some pretty tender times in my life, having a photo of me as a nine-year-old has helped me to be extra supportive of and compassionate toward the little one in me. When I am triggered as an adult, I can go back and remember that it is my inner child who requires some validation. So when I see her on the altar, I send her love and my heart opens because she is so sweet and beautiful. Back when I was little, I may not have gotten all of my needs met, or felt like I didn't have a voice. But today, I can heal that energy within me by sending that little girl who is within me so much understanding and love.

Remember that the objects you place on your altar don't have to have any meaning to anybody else. This is your personal healing time and space. Perhaps you have seashells, jewelry, dried flowers, figurines, or tokens that are of significance to you. These things can help us connect to the deepest part of who we are because they hold the energy of time inside. As we sit in front of our shrine, which is another name for an altar, these objects that are sacred to us can support us in connecting with our spiritual side, with family members present or ancestors passed, and our guides, and assist us in our moment-to-moment spiritual evolution.

ALTAR RITUALS

There are three meaningful mainstays of my altar that I want to offer you, three rituals for enlivening your altar.

First, if you have access to them, I suggest placing freshly cut flowers on your shrine. Their fragrance represents our pure innocence and inner beauty. We learn so much from our cut flowers as we see them wilt over time. Impermanence reminds us that we are only here for a short time and that our body, just like our flowers, will one day return to the earth. As we witness impermanence, it can help us remember our life's purpose and be inspired by who we are, beautiful human beings given only so much time on this precious earth.

Second, I recommend lighting a candle and placing it on your altar. The light of a candle evokes a sense of longing to know ourselves from a deeper place within us. Not just on a surface level or only through our intellect, but to really see and feel our deep light inside, our "insight," which is the truest part of who we are. This light is beyond our knowledge, free of gender and any other identity. This wisdom is known from within us, and through the candle's light, any darkness evaporates, and we see ourselves more clearly.

Third, I suggest lighting some incense that you find fragrant. The burning of incense brings a freshness of color, beauty, and imagination to our minds and our homes by helping us to connect our spirit with our sensual body. The smoke (spirit) enters our nose (body), sanctifying and purifying both.

We are walking, explosive, exalted states of energy and yet very human at the same time. Everything in our altar, whether it's the Buddha, the candle you light, or the fresh flowers that you placed there from your garden, is infused with this energy. The altar can be a place that ignites your deepest creative purpose that you were put here to give to yourself and the world. I have a Mother Mary, Jesus, and Buddha statue on mine, and I change what I put there from day to day depending on what is important to me. If I am having a hard time with someone, I'll sometimes place their photo on the shrine and try to be with them and forgive myself and them. This practice isn't easy for me, but I guess I've come to the point where I just want to be so free that I am willing to be with the difficult things.

Sometimes, when I sit in front of my shrine, I will say a few words of prayer that go like this:

It is my intention to connect deeply with who I really am, and in sitting here, I am reminded of this deeper part of me. And that I will be safe in all that I do. Dear Universe, it is my intention to give love and be love to myself and all beings. Also, I will be open to

receiving love in all that I do, and all things that I am today. Thank you, dear Universe, for providing all that I need and in the exact way that helps me live life in this physical world. It is my intention that I enjoy the material world, and that my needs are met, but that I don't allow myself to be seduced by greed and lose sight of real love above anything else. This is my mission statement for the day, and these are the words that feel true to me and help me feel divinely connected with Source. Love is necessary. It is our evolution. May all beings meet this moment not only with the intelligence of the brain or the intellect in the mind but with the expanded intelligence of our human heart. Let us connect with our hearts, dear ones, and may all sentient beings have a beautiful day filled with the love of the universe that is not just outside of us but something that is resting deeply in each one of us too.

Saying these words or making up your own while being present in your sacred place is essential for a deeper connection with ourselves and with all beings we share this planet with. At any time or hour of the day when you're home and you feel disturbed, you can go there, even if it's in the middle of the night. When my household is up and running for the day, I can sometimes feel distracted from my inner life—or what's probably truer is that my role as mom and homemaker takes over, and it's easy to forget my spiritual nature. So if you share your home with others, take advantage of the time either early in the morning or later at night once your people (and your animals!) are in bed, and come to a place of peace and quietude in front of your altar.

When we tap into this place of peace and quietude, it doesn't just stay in our home in front of our altar, but we take its energy with us. Sometimes you may literally need to take a piece of your altar with you— perhaps when you are traveling, you can pack something/s from your altar and set it up wherever you are visiting, so you can recall its energy. I'll usually bring some favorite incense from home and after lighting it, just those few scent-waves help me to remember my peaceful and quiet nature within. Maybe you have a battery-operated candle that travels easily and that you feel safe leaving on when you're away. Or maybe it's a photograph or another transportable object like a crystal. You can also bring something of your altar with you to your office, if you work away from home, or carry a small sacred token with you at all times in your purse or pocket.

THE ALTAR WITHIN

I've been talking about an exterior altar in your home, or tangible objects you carry with you into your life beyond the home, but there's also an inner altar we all carry, a scared place we can tap into inside, with the help of our bodies, to bring ourselves back into peace and quietude, the place where we can hear our own inner wisdom.

I am turning 48 this year and as I move into middle age and closer to menopause, I notice physical changes are happening. I have noticed lately that I wake up sporadically throughout the night. And if I don't go to my phone first, which is helpful not to do, I'll go into my inner place and space and just sit for a few moments. Sometimes, I'll light a real candle, sit, and do some stretches, and usually, I can go back to sleep when I feel ready. In the past, I would say to myself, "Oh you just have to force yourself to go back to sleep because your day is going to be horrible otherwise," but that was my conditioning and thought patterns before I realized there was another way. Practicing meditation or being in a restorative yogic-like position, laying down, and placing a few pillows underneath our knees, and focusing on our breath can sometimes feel like the same amount of restful sleep we would have gotten. If I listen to my conditioning or feel limited by it, then I feel stuck and imprisoned laying in my bed trying to will myself back to sleep. But I know that if I just get up, shift the energy, and allow for more rest to happen, things usually evolve into a positive back-to-sleep kind of way.

I find that early mornings are an especially good time to visit the altar within in a ritualistic way.

 If it's possible, I suggest you wake naturally and give yourself some time for gentle reflection and meditation. The mind hasn't yet formed huge thoughts, and our awareness is wide open. Laying down, and perhaps even hearing the bird song outside, we can become aware of our breath. We are alert, but not yet active. It's a gentle way to "feel in" to our dreams and set a peaceful tone for the day. I love the vast boundaryless realm within me that is a place where I feel safe and settled.

This space is for me alone, to imagine, dream big, and love. In these moments, a fertile garden is growing the seeds of my awareness. And what is possible, or not possible, is up to me and me alone. This time breeds creativity and allows for my heart and soul to integrate. Feeling and emulating this kind of calm and integration is a great foundation for the rest of the day.

When I spend time in the sacred space inside the deepest part of me and feel my connection with the divine source, anything is possible. It's a "knowing" feeling, and it comes from practicing and living in awareness. Anything that we need is already inside of us, especially the things that we yearn for. Those things are beating within our own hearts, just waiting for us to take their hand. I like reminding myself that anything that I'd wish to experience is only a breath away and is never outside of myself. Each day, we have the opportunity to build this kind of connection and trust within us and in our sacred place. The positive energy of our feelings in this internal room accumulates, and we can feel hopeful, positive energy every time we visit. We can connect to the deepest part of who we are, and this space is a physical manifestation of it.

Essentially, we could say that an external altar is the outside manifestation of what is already inside of you, your internal altar. The time you spend in both places and the devotion in your heart will just keep becoming stronger every day. You'll tap into and expand your inner resources, and guidance from your deep intuitive heart will lead your life. When we lead from our heart, we are open and less judgmental of ourselves and others, and we seem to live with more overall happiness. This is the promise of cultivating a prayerful awareness.

LOVING OURSELF WITH AWARENESS

If you are having an intense moment, just remember that none of us have it all worked out. Some of us are just trying to get through the day and continue to work on self-love.

What does it mean to truly love ourselves? Why is it so important? And how do we get there?

The Buddha said, "If your compassion does not include yourself, it is incomplete." But is self-compassion the same as self-love? We know it's good for us, but how many of us really give ourselves compassion? If we want to achieve a higher level of personal development, which includes real happiness and inner peace, then being able to have compassion for all people must include ourselves.

On my best days, before saying a word or doing anything, I'll stop and pause and say, *What would love do?* What would the grandmother energy—the wise voice in all of us—inside me say/feel/respond? At the very least, she would love me fiercely and love all of me unconditionally.

If one of the biggest tasks in life is to understand who we really are, what if truly loving ourselves is the key to this understanding? To look back on my own life struggles with mental health issues, low self-esteem, and a lack of inner connection, I might be able to narrow it down to a lack of self-love. Self-love isn't the kind of love that is selfish, egotistical, or cheesy. This is the hugely underrated path to real happiness, inner peace, and a life worth living.

Without a doubt, true self-love helps us to explore and go after our dreams in life. When we love and accept ourselves, we understand that falling down and making mistakes are all part of being human. We learn, grow, and don't waste any time with negative thoughts.

Without self-love and acceptance, we may…

- self-sabotage and deprive ourselves of "good" relationships because "normal" can feel boring and not what we're used to
- be cruel to ourselves and not just think harmful thoughts, but worse, believe them!
- develop unrealistic expectations for ourselves and others
- take things personally and take on every little insecurity felt by other people as if it's our own
- make up unrealistic and sometimes bizarre scenarios or stories about ourselves and others
- neglect and sometimes cause harm to our bodies because those stories we've always told ourselves to keep us small can be so loud and believable

SEVEN PRAYERFUL INTENTIONS FOR CREATING MORE LOVING AND ACCEPTING RELATIONSHIPS WITH OURSELVES

1. **Let us view our behaviors that don't favor and foster self-love in a non-judgmental and compassionate way.** By recognizing old behavioral patterns that perhaps we needed for survival purposes, we might have a chance of transmuting negative behaviors into self-love and acceptance. By becoming even just a little bit more aware of the moments when we live on autopilot, we can bring ourselves back to who we are, the magnificent drivers of our own destiny. It might be easy for us to think that Betty down the street is doing great because we only see her accomplishments. We

might go into victim mode and feel "less than," or even envious because we are not where we think Betty is. The truth is, we can never compare ourselves to someone else—not even yourself from last week could compete with you today! We are all so unique and come with our own magic. We are here to discover what that magic is and share it with those around us. May we practice honest self-reflection so we are able to be more objective with ourselves and with what shows up in our lives. When we do have some control, may we be gentle with ourselves, because so often we disturb our inner balance. When we're having an intense moment, just remember that none of us have it all worked out, not even Betty down the street.

2. **Let us do the inner work that comes with befriending the parts within us we may wish we never developed.** Once we do this, we hold these parts in a safe place in our hearts. Imagine a beloved child runs to us in pain, maybe from having fallen down. If we are connected to our inner selves, then we are more likely to respond with compassion. We are less likely to tell them they shouldn't feel sad or hurt or need to "shrug it off." Instead, we would look them in the eye and validate what they are feeling. Our emotions can sometimes be like little children asking for our attention. If we respond with kindness, the child feels seen, heard, and knows from a deep place that the world is safe. That if we fall down, we are held in grace, and not shame or blame like a lot of us developed in our childhood.

3. **Let us learn lessons from those around us.** I'm always so amazed at how the universe seems to bring in the best person at the right time for me to learn more about myself. Best doesn't always mean comfortable, by the way. For me, when I am uncomfortable inside a relationship, I understand that there are valuable lessons for me to learn. For instance, if we understand that our relationships are much less about making us happy and are more about assisting us to become more conscious, we see our relationships as another pathway toward self-realization and self-understanding, and we generally can then let go of any expectations for the other.

Forgiveness, acceptance, and self-compassion always seem to be the most important lessons. I know if I am feeling triggered inside a relationship, I need to slow down and bring in a huge amount of self-compassion. After I feel the self-compassion running through my body and heart, I add some forgiveness for going down whatever emotional tunnel I needed to in the moment to understand more about myself. Then I wholeheartedly accept myself for where I'm at, inside and out. This is all very human stuff. We can learn so much about ourselves when we employ a child-like wonder about the folks that are drawn into our lives. Our so-called flaws only want to be loved like a tree in the forest: we would never say that a tree in the forest is too big or too leafy, we look at it in awe and love it, just as it is. We are more than enough. We're thankful for other people who remind us of this important lesson.

4. **Let us understand that becoming triggered by someone can be a real gift**, but only if we choose to see it that way. Being able to gently point the finger back inside to take some responsibility for any part of getting triggered is life-changing and healing. Usually, we spend much more time blaming others instead of forgiving ourselves and moving into a self-compassionate way of being. When we spend years pointing the finger away from us, our mental and physical health, relationships, and careers suffer. In effect, we are refusing the gift of an opportunity to forgive ourselves and others, denying the wounded humanity that resides in us all that can only be healed by love.

5. **Let us take good care of our bodies.** We commit to preparing healthy meals, going for walks, and getting our environment organized so we set ourselves up for a successful day. The body is our heart's home; it is our soul's vehicle to help us understand more about ourselves. If we treat it with respect, we are better able to turn down the volume of the inner critic and choose to be a positive change-maker in life. Our body is not separate from the life we are living. It can be our best ally! Always listen to gut feelings. If something feels off, it is. If something feels right, it is. Never doubt our inner GPS system—it is our best navigational tool in life. In listening more deeply to its cues, loving, and accepting it, everyone around us benefits.

6. **Let us spend time alone being present with an energy of self-love.** We begin gently in the morning by doing things that connect us with our highest selves, be it meditation, affirmations, devotional reading, stretching, or sipping our coffee mindfully. These acts of self-love will set the tone for our day. This could take less than ten minutes, so it's important not to allow our minds to talk us out of this special time to connect with what's most important to us. We book-end our days with some loving acts for ourselves too, like time spent in front of our altars, a stroll to unwind from the day's energy, or relaxing in a body of water. We don't multitask, as these times are not meant for completing anything else on our to-do lists. When we love someone, we want to spend time with them alone—when we love ourselves, we feel the same way.

7. **Let us learn to give and receive love more consciously.** If we have been abused, neglected, or abandoned by ourselves or others, receiving can be challenging, but it's important that we see ourselves as worthy of our own love, and also worthy of love from others. The folks in our lives are not necessarily there to make our lives better—that's up to us—but if that's something they desire to do, we can learn to accept their love with grace and gratitude. If we notice that it's hard to receive love from the people in our life, be it a smile, a hug, or whatever, we practice just gently witnessing our reaction. If we are always the giver, it can mean that we slowly leak out energy, and might often feel tired, especially around the folks we are giving to. There may be a martyr's energy within us rearing its head if we are not careful. I have noticed that when I care for those I love, the little one inside of me that wasn't seen and heard as a child can ride high on their admiration. Most of us want to do a good job when we do something, but to be always looking for validation might mean we have some inner-child work to explore. Sometimes we have to ask ourselves deep questions like, "What part of me is doing the giving right now? Is it my heart that needs nothing in return, or is it my ego overcompensating for a lack of love that I could be giving myself?" On the receiving end of the spectrum, we might ask ourselves something like, "What part of me is not seeing myself as worthy of all the good coming into my life?" We don't want to block what the universe is trying

to give to us, which is like the sun and doesn't discriminate who or what it shines its light on.

LIVING INTENTIONALLY WITH AWARENESS

"Our intention creates our reality."
— *Wayne Dyer*

Have you ever wondered what intention-setting is all about, and why it's so important? An intention is simply an idea that you plan to carry out, manifest, or work toward. It is a collection of focused energy that turns your attention to your own awareness and deepest desires. It's based in the present moment while it gazes toward the future. Intentions hold dreams, hopes, and for many of us, things that we wish to happen, hopefully for our highest good and the highest good of others.

Intention-setting requires that we direct our energy to that which is most meaningful to us. We become more consciously aware of where we are directing our energy. As we direct our energy to that which is meaningful, we feel connected to our highest purpose. When we are living in our highest purpose, it doesn't matter so much what the activity is as much as how the activity is carried out. We seek alignment in our hearts, body, spirit, and mind in carrying out our intentions.

Most folks who run a business understand the value and necessity of setting goals, but I wonder how many set intentions? The difference between goal setting and intention-setting is that goals have more of an emphasis on the future and can take us out of the moment, focusing on what we don't have. Setting intentions allows us to focus on who we are in the moment, and to value what is good and working well already. When we value what we have, we open ourselves up to more of that positive energy to come to us. It also raises our vibration, our emotional and physical energy. As everything we need is already inside of us and can manifest on the outside too, valuing what we already have helps us to heal, grow, and live in abundance.

Intentions, if used wisely, can give us inspiration that supports our daily choices. Setting intentions daily, and not waiting for when life gets a little rocky, is preventive, which is much better than treatment. They can also help us to be less distracted when life throws us these curve balls, and not to spend too much time acting out a life that is not in alignment with who we really are.

How can we honor the past and all that has happened and also move into being the best we can be right now? The current moment usually dictates the next moment's energy. This is why daily intentions are a good way to honor the moment or to create new moments where something more in alignment with our souls can happen. Sometimes, I will create an intention for a specific experience in my day. It could be something like knocking out my housecleaning tasks early in the day so I can tend to my writing, or going to the grocery store and coming home safely with nutritious food to feed my family. In these examples, cleaning the house and running errands are mere goals, but you can see the deeper intentions behind them—in the former, to make time to foster my creativity, and in the latter, to take good care of my family. To fortify my intentions, I might light a real candle or, if I am pressed for time, I will light one in my heart, close my eyes, and imagine the light there. I might say something like, "May I please be looked after as I clean the house or run off to the store, and may no obstacles make their way on my path. May my actions today serve my creativity and my family well."

I also feel quite centered within myself when I make time for setting intentions. I feel purposeful and powerful. This doesn't mean that what I intend to happen will be guaranteed to happen—none of us are that powerful! The other side of intention-setting is allowing for things to be as they will be. I feel deeply that one of the secrets in life is accepting what happens inside of it. Like if good things happen, so be it, if bad things happen, so be it, if neutral things happen, so be it. This radical acceptance has the potential to assist us in feeling more peaceful and grounded. Meaning, we make our intentions and feel them in our bones and, at the same time, we allow for life to unfold in its own time and manner.

We might imagine that the universe has its own intentions as well, and while it's lovely when its intentions are in alignment with ours, that won't always be the case. The universe may send me a friend in need who calls when I'm cleaning the house, and I know the right thing to do is to willingly sacrifice my creative time to care for her. I may see a lost dog on the side of the road on my way to the grocery store, and I know the universe is tasking me with making sure I get him safely to a shelter, knowing my family will have to settle for some healthy take-out food in lieu of a home-cooked meal.

But these kind of sacrifices are only right if I feel I have enough energy in my heart, physical body, and energetic field in that moment. If I don't actually have the space within me to care for another, it might be that the best thing I can do for the other (and especially me) is to not get involved at all. This might come across as selfish or cruel, but in the end, if we are not genuinely understanding our own needs first, how can we be authentically there for another? We risk hurting ourselves if we go above and beyond what we are physically, emotionally, and energetically able to give.

Whether we live with and set intentions or not, life does seem to be a continuum of holding on and letting go—holding on to what is most important and meaningful while letting go and accepting our life "as it is." Once we accept life on its own terms, we don't mind all of the disturbances inside of it—*that's just life*, we tell ourselves. And the mind is less likely to jump from black to white, good to bad, and right to wrong—we don't think to ourselves, my intention was right, and the way things turned out is wrong. It simply just *is what it is*. We are co-creators *with* the universe, not creators *of* the universe. So if you feel frustrated like your intentions are always or often blocked, try looking at how you can come to terms with what is right here in front of you.

Also, try not to be in a rush to get all your intentions fulfilled because something tells me this is a lifelong journey, and that's okay. What a beautiful life it is when we open it up to a more intentional way of living.

 In your journal, contemplate questions like, where am I in my life? And what is my mind, body, and spirit really trying to tell me? We need to be our best advocates, and best listeners, and connect into our hearts with honest investigation. This can often take time, but more importantly, your own awareness, to make the time to be with you. Any time of year, day, week, and month is a great time to do this, yet we often use the New Year to reflect on how we would like to live our best lives and to set our intentions.

For most of his time with his son, the Buddha was a single dad. He often said to his son: "Use your actions as a mirror to reflect where you're at in your life." This advice translates to me as . . . *Not only do our words matter, but so do our behavior and motivations.* But here's the catch— we usually respond to life with actions and behaviors that stem from the way we have been programmed or conditioned. This is why practicing yoga, meditation, and mindfulness can be such good tools for re-conditioning ourselves. Positive affirmations are also effective, as we can actually reprogram our thought patterns by repeating positive and life-giving sound bites.

We have all experienced the power of gratitude. When we do practice gratitude, it can often take our minds off our problems and perceived limitations. For example, if I voice an intention that I wish to live in gratitude for all that I am and for all that I have, joy and love fill up my heart and body with positive energy. As cheesy as it might sound, for many of us, it works!

We can also imbue our rituals with intentions. Do you have a gentle ritual like making your tea, coffee, or water with lemon that helps to ground, restore, and honor who you are? I know that when I wake and offer myself some warm water with lemon and speak a simple intention

like, *May it be nourished with the vibration of love*, I feel much more connected to myself. I feel grounded, restored, and know that even in a
turbulent world, I can nourish my inner sanctum and the outer spaces
I'm living in.

NEW MOON RITUAL

 Working with the new moon is a wonderful way for us
to sync our body's rhythm with that of the universe. According to practitioners of moon mapping, the new
moon is a time for us to ask important questions to our
higher self, or to discover bigger aspirations that we
could work toward in the following thirty days of the
lunar cycle. It is a time when we are invited to set new intentions and
think about what we might be open to learning and receiving, and what
we are wanting to work on. This is a time when we are planting seeds
for the future. During this time, it can feel and look as though the light
has been taken from the night sky. The moon is very small, and by
placing a seed of intention within our hearts, we can watch it germi-
nate. That little seed of intention will eventually begin to grow.

What I love about the new moon is that it is a time for us to understand
ourselves a little better, by slowing down and checking in with ourselves. Even if you don't "believe" in astrology, you can partake in a
new moon ritual, knowing that just like us, the moon is beautiful and
exactly where it is meant to be. The new moon quite simply can help
support us in where we are right now and where we are wanting to go.
In a new moon ritual, we ask ourselves questions like "What am I ready
to invite in?" and "What is my soul yearning to do?" We plant our
intention like a seed in the garden of our hearts and dreams. During
the first three days of the new moon, the sky is dark, yet the seeds of
intention have been sown, and we just need to be patient as they begin
to grow.

What kinds of intentions can we set? It could be something creative
like starting a new hobby or having an intention around receiving and
being more peaceful. Our intention could even be all about getting
back on track, about becoming more in alignment with our soul and
the rhythm of life. Or it could be about starting a new physical exercise

or eating program. The bigger things in life are often on the top of our list, like bringing in a job that is in better alignment with who we are, or finding a partner if we are single. We may set our intention on others, on a situation, a person, or even a country that might need an extra boost and our loving-kindness. We can set our intention for simple things that are just as wonderful for us, like wanting to begin a meditation practice, or stretch our body more, even an intention of making more time to connect with our family and friends. A new moon intention could even be something deep and spiritual, like expanding our minds in the field of knowing and consciousness.

After placing your new moon intention in your heart, it's good to let go of what the outcome looks like, and your ideas of how it should be fulfilled. The universe may surprise you, so if you have a feeling that you should do something, but you don't know exactly why, it's good to trust it. It could be as silly as going to the grocery store and picking up coconut milk for a recipe that your body is craving to make and eat. If you listen and go, you could bump into someone that you haven't seen in a while and end up reconnecting with them in some way that fulfills your intention. After the new moon, don't only look for outside confirmation to lead you in the direction of your intention; remember that sometimes it's having the courage to follow your intuition that helps you on your truest path. I love the poet Rumi's idea that what we seek is also seeking us. I feel comfort in these words because if the intention we've put into the universe really is in alignment with our soul's growth, it will one day come to us. The key though is to be uber-patient. Though we may doubt it, divine timing really will work its magic, and whatever we need will come to us when we are ready for it.

That doesn't mean that we sit around passively waiting for our intentions to manifest—we need to signal to the universe that we're active co-creators with it through our actions. For example, if your intention is to meet new people, then maybe that looks like signing up for a specific club or gym. If your intention is to deepen your spiritual practice, that might look like signing up for a retreat, or researching spiritual teachers in your area. Be ready to support your intention by making the necessary steps in getting closer to it, and then allow the magic to unfold.

If we are not internally ready for something that we have asked for, then we need to believe in ourselves and do the work. That might mean creating an affirmation that is specific to our intention. Let's say you are looking for a loving partner. Perhaps you might create an affirmation to recite throughout the day like, "I am already enough and am attracting a fulfilling relationship into my life that is balanced and supportive of who I am." Don't just say the words, but feel them within the body, a feeling that runs so deep in you that you become the magnet for that same energy to come into your life. Feel it so much in your body that you begin to "see," or visualize, it. For example, you may close your eyes throughout the day and imagine yourself holding this special someone in your arms, or picking up groceries together, or perhaps even doing something mundane like folding the laundry together. Make the connection to your mind, heart, and body that this person, this feeling, and this understanding is with you now.

Then, at the same time, be proactive. If a friend says they have someone in mind for you, perhaps make the effort to meet them. Or join a community with people who share your interests. Maybe it's a book club, or a meditation and yoga community. You could even do online dating. Do the steps that it takes to get yourself out there. Don't be the person who only hears their intuition, but be the person who listens and takes action around it too.

I also suggest that you write your intentions down, perhaps in your journal, or on a note card you place on your altar. Then you can look back on your new moon journey and see what you have been able to intentionally bring into your life. I did this with the love of my life who is now my husband and the father of our two teens. I had been married twice before so I knew that I needed the right fit for who I am. I wrote out about 20 things that really stood out for me that I would like in a partner. I kid you not, he showed up within a year of getting clear and writing this out. I still have the list to this day and often refer to it with a chuckle. The only advice I would give is to be really clear, be rested when writing things down, and don't sell yourself short. You are worthy of great love if this is indeed something you would like. And you are worthy of a partner who is supportive, who meets you where you are today, and who can be with you as you grow throughout the years.

COOKING AS AN INTENTIONAL RITUAL

A big part of my own healing practice is caretaking "little Mellara," my inner child within. When I do this, everyone in my life seems to benefit. If you are like me and grew up in a household that didn't always feel safe, it's especially important to take care of your little one. One way I do this is through cooking. It almost feels like cooking and preparing food allows for a kind of nurturing that is similar to being our own parent or friend. It's such a beautiful practice.

I didn't always used to like cooking and the inevitable cleaning afterwards. Even now, on some days when I don't feel connected to my truest nature, I can feel resentment about it. On those days, I remind myself that the most challenging yoga posture or hike has nothing on the harmony that is created when we focus on what matters most—in this example, nurturing little Mellara. With this devotional act of cooking, all of who I am comes together, my past and present self, with love. Even the most mundane aspects of life, like cooking and cleaning, can help us become more whole, and live in deeper awareness.

May we feed all aspects of who we are through preparing, cooking, cleaning, and see our healthy bodies as a foundation for the gifts we offer the world.

When I was in my 20s, I saw a nutritionist who also offered colonics as part of her services. It was the most healing thing I could have done for myself during this time of my life. I was learning what fueled my body best and what kept my mind, body, and soul balanced. She invited me to be accountable for what I ate during the day by writing it all down in a journal. She said, "Always, please Mellara, have one big salad every day with all the different colors of the rainbow inside of it for vegetables." I didn't realize it back then, but I was practicing mindfulness as I jotted down the foods that I ate and kept myself accountable for what I was eating. Another way I practiced mindfulness then and still now is in the chopping and touching of the food. I say a quick little prayer to all the hands that were involved in making these ingredients available for me to eat and stay nourished. Cooking our food is also a mindful exercise that helps our mind to relax. Perhaps we start off listening to a podcast or music to soothe and calm the body as we prepare our food, and then, one day, we might decide we just want to relish the sounds of gathering, washing, cutting, and assembling whatever food is being prepared.

I have a ritual around cooking lentils and rice for the new moon. It helps me to feel healthy and if I haven't been giving my body all the nutrients it needs, I know that at least every new moon when I cook the lentils and rice, I have the opportunity to begin all over again. Do you have a dish that brings comfort to your heart, mind, and body that you would like to cook at the new moon? Perhaps it's an old family recipe that you'd like to revive and bring back into your life, or a recipe you've stashed away for someday, and that someday is now. When we cook as a ritual it can support us in feeling good, peaceful, and satisfied. The act of cooking is a creative outlet in itself. If cooking just isn't your thing, perhaps it is going out to your favorite restaurant or bringing home take-out. Stay open-minded about the rituals you would like to experience around the new moon. It's not something that we can really get wrong as it is unique to each one of us.

INTENTIONALLY INCREASING OUR FREQUENCY

Everything in the universe, including you and me, is frequency. It feels important to know this, because if we do, then we have the power to merge with other energy sources. We kind of do it anyway, like when we join a group for a coffee, have Thanksgiving with our family, or go to a yoga class. But why is it important to know this? Because all energy is in constant motion, can't ever be stopped, and can only be changed or transformed into something else.

I believe that if each one of us who is operating at a frequency of love can elevate our consciousness, other folks operating at lower energies can feel these positive effects. It's like the monk who has been meditating in a cave his whole life. An outsider might say that he isn't really doing too much for society as a whole, but the extension of his positive and loving energy into the world is indeed the supportive energy we need to heal division, separation, and hate.

Being loving, kind, and living in awareness seems to be the answer. As we practice meditation, walk in nature, and tune into our beingness or spirit, we tune in to the frequency of love. To feel our best selves and set our day in motion, it helps to do things we love, even something as small as listening to our favorite music. It's important that we expose ourselves to the frequencies that harmonize with us.

As we are vibrational beings living in a vibrational universe, we naturally attract similar frequencies of who we are. The universe is not out to get us. Even with the most personal of things that happen in our lives, we can consider it all vibration. The universe responds to the vibration that we are, and not necessarily what we ask for. We receive unfailingly whatever it is that our vibration frequency requests or is open to. This is why it is important to have simple practices that can drop us into our hearts, and to what is most important to us, which may be presence, love, and joy. The universe picks up on our vibrational frequency and attracts to us that which reflects the same vibration that is within us.

Our emotional body is designed to receive vibrations, but also to "transmit" these vibrations out, where they are then picked up and reflected back to us in concrete ways. So this can mean that if we have unresolved issues around any kind of abuse, for instance, our body can emit a vibration that might attract more of the same energy in different forms, people, and life situations. Our abuse is part of our vibration, but in doing work around it to heal, we can transform its energy. The universe is on our side in this venture.

RITUALS TO RAISE OUR VIBRATIONS

1. Remind yourself in the early hours of the morning that you are not alone, that you are what you have been searching for, and that you are divine energy, God, nature, or whatever word you resonate with the most.

2. Witness your thoughts—don't always believe them or take them so personally. Catch yourself if you get stuck in a loop of negative

thought patterns and bring yourself back to your feeling body and breath.

3. Find something around you that connects you to the natural world and be with it. Maybe it's a flower in the garden or holding a seashell, rock, or crystal.

4. Give your body occasional breaks from sugar and eat foods that your body finds easier to digest.

5. Drink at least eight glasses of water a day.

6. Meditate in the shower or bath and feel the energy that the water is giving you.

7. Practice gratitude for things you do have in your life, and you'll see that the more you are in this energy, the more that energy will come back to you. And if possible, try not to focus on what you don't have. Being grateful for the breath, grateful that your body is being breathed, is a wonderful start.

8. Be kind to yourself and honor if you need a "rest day" or even a few hours to just be with yourself in a park. Your body will tell you what it needs through how it feels. If you feel tired or exhausted, it's time to listen to your body and respect what it is trying to tell you. Our body understands so much more than we give it credit for.

9. Move your body and keep it in motion with something that expresses the spirit within you. It could be dancing in your living room, singing in the shower, or having a deep belly laugh over a silly video.

10. Say uplifting affirmations. You could start with "My vibration is moving to new heights with every moment."

11. Go on a news and electronics detox from time to time.

12. Refrain from persuading others to join you or to think and feel as you do. This is your practice and others will simply benefit by being in your presence as you make the necessary changes that feel positive to you.

May we bring more intentionality into living with awareness.

GLOSSARY

asana: yoga poses to open the body.

ahankara: the self that is "doing" or "acting" or the personality associated with the individual body. Referring to the sense of being an individual separate from everything else.

being: effortless flow.

beingness: non-doing presence.

chitta: all that is perceived and all that can be perceived. Chitta allows for subjectivity, and one's emotional reaction that is affected by what it sees and its own nature.

consciousness: awareness.

ego: everyday mind, self-identity.

guides: spirit beings that assist in life's journey.

higher consciousness: immersion in transcendence.

intellect: problem-solving capacity of the mind.

intuition: understanding viscerally, without the need for reasoning; also, *intuitive intelligence*.

manas: the perceptive mind, or how the world appears through the instruments of the senses.

mantra: a sound repeated to help us connect with ourselves and to a deeper reality.

metta: unconditional love and loving-kindness.

mind: a set of cognitive faculties including consciousness, imagination, perception, thinking, judgment, language, and memory. The term *mind* is usually used in living in awareness practice to mean an out-of-control, small mind.

Mother Gaia: goddess of earth and mother of all life.

no self: the Buddha's teaching that there is no permanent, autonomous self.

path: journey toward realization which is unique to every individual.

practice: meditation, yoga, or engaging the teachings in everyday life.

prayerful: as an act of being self-reflective and self-exanimating. It can also be seen as being devout.

soul: the spiritual or immaterial aspect of being.

true nature: being-nature, the fundamental capacity of all beings to live inside an awakened presence.

unconscious: not conscious.

witnessing: observing your own life neutrally, without affect; being present and noticing, not judging.

yoga: literally "union" of the individual with divine consciousness; a spiritual discipline that includes breath control, meditation, and postures, widely practiced for health and wellness.

yoga nidra: state of consciousness between waking and sleeping; deep relaxation.

A FINAL NOTE FROM THE AUTHOR

Dear Reader,

I hope in some small way this book offers support to you on your life journey. And may we all remember that peace in our world is essentially an extension of the peace we have within us. Chipping away at self-discovery while being mindful feels like a good path toward a more peaceful, just, kind, and inclusive world. In the end, it's our hearts that would love us to come back to ourselves, not to lift up and puff out, but to drop in, trust, and anchor. This is such a profound time because humanity is coming to a precipice. Now, having lived through turbulence, a pandemic, and now Putin's war in Ukraine, more of us seem to be waking up. With the outside world feeling chaotic, we seem to be experiencing a grand transformation, and with all of this movement and change, our life can understandably feel uncertain at times.

If we could just make some small steps to move, think, and arrange our lives toward more awareness of the simple things, we might discover a sense of wholeness along the way. To me, wholeness asks me to be open to and be more accepting of myself as I am. That means my body's shape, my life's circumstances, and anything that usually pops up on any given day. Yet this doesn't mean we become complacent; it actually means we can become more aware of what we need while listening to that quiet voice within—not the louder judgmental voice, but the calm and kind voice that comes to visit us when we make the time to be with ourselves. All we can do is our best by being uber-kind to ourselves, by giving our body healthy foods, being active, and speaking to ourselves as we would to a dear friend. Wholeness is not about being perfect, it is instead about seeing ourselves as a work in progress. We may have some things that we would like to change about ourselves, but at our core, we feel all right in the world because we feel all right within. Wholeness is loving ourselves for who we are and not some future self that is only made up in our minds.

When I published my memoir at the end of 2021, I felt it to be one small part of this larger movement toward wholeness of mind, body, and spirit. Even if it's only my story, every time any of us becomes more aware and more loving toward ourselves, the world is much closer to peace. My book, *A Life Worth Living,* follows my early life with a tumultuous upbringing and how I came to understand myself by self-discovery, healing, mindfulness, yoga, and living in awareness. It's about how, in the end, life itself is our biggest teacher, lesson, and classroom. To be whole begins with understanding who we are and where we get caught up or fractured, and not being hard on ourselves when we inevitably do. We are going to make mistakes, and it's how we speak to ourselves when we do that makes all the difference. With loving and mindful awareness, we bring the fractured pieces together, embrace them, and heal those areas that have caused us and others more harm than good. I explore these ideas in my book through the lens of my personal story.

In the 20th century, we have made spectacular advances in the sciences and technology, and we're now able to live in much more comfort and ease. Many diseases have been eradicated, communication has become instantaneous, and travel around the world is almost lightning-fast. Un-fortunately, many of these advantages were obtained using energy sources that have fouled the planet and caused more diseases to pro-liferate. It's time to clean up our mess—to stop our destructive habits, mitigate environmental degradation, and use only renewable resources as sources of power. We need to return to life in balance. 2020 espe-cially was a big year of this reminder, as though the Earth Goddess Gaia herself intervened.

This century is an opportunity for us to grow ecologically and spiritually. Having benefited from industrialization, technology, transportation, and the digital revolution, we need to re-learn peace, stewardship, and sustainability. Instead of only reaching outward for our next discoveries, we need to return within, reconnect with our hearts, and recognize the beings of light that we are. After a millennium of being anesthetized from feeling our joy or our pain, it is time for us to heal ourselves and our Mother Earth. If each of us takes one small step toward living in awareness, change on a grand scale is possible.

Living in awareness is neither strict nor lax but encourages us to be open to what is. I've learned that true freedom is indestructible. We are human *and* holy, small yet powerful, alone and at the same time a part of all the stars of the universe. May you take refuge in all of who you are, your inner and outer beauty, and know that you are a very important part of our world. The reason we know this is that you are here now! We need you and all that you offer our world, and sometimes it is only our presence that is needed the most.

Having a practice of connecting with ourselves every day leads to the realization that we are loved dearly and not separate from anything. At times you might spend alone time with yourself but remember that this is different from being alone or lonely. Alone time is when we are connected to our heart, while feeling lonely just might mean that we have listened to and believed too many self-defeating thoughts. If we can drop down and into the heart space, we can explore and find more ways to comfort our precious hearts. We are not just worthy of our own self-exploration and love, but our survival as a species seems to be dependent on it. Wounded people may consciously or unconsciously wound others and wound the planet, but people on a path of healing may offer abundant love to themselves, others, and Mother Gaia.

I'm not sure that our life will ever get "easy" as we live here on Earth school, as I like to call it. Life will probably do whatever life wants to do. But all is not lost as we find simple ways to love the life we are in, celebrate ourselves, and let go of any striving to be successful in a material sense. Not that having money is actually bad for us—it is a very important part of life—but our society has made us feel we have to achieve certain milestones on a timeline. It's time that we live as our soul feels is right for us, not our bank account. There is no better time to show up as a sovereign in our lives than right now. This is about feeling and being empowered in all that we are and not about asserting power over another. Being our own sovereign self gives us access to who we are at a soul level, so we don't always have to be looking for a group to validate us because we have this feeling or knowing deep within us.

There were many seasons in my life where I followed what others said over what I knew to be true. Some of it was important for my development, and listening to leaders who are inspiring feels amazing, but at the end of the day, they are inside their bodies and we are inside ours. May we become more understanding that our sovereignty is about standing up for our beliefs and trusting in the wisdom that we have learned, and earned, along the way. And while it may seem easy to read this, it could very well be a practice we continue throughout our whole life. Our life is the practice room as we learn, fall down, and get back up again along the way. It's not *if* we are going to fall, it's *when* and *how*, and it's not even about the fall as much as it's about how we rise again. How can we respond rather than react? We don't necessarily need to figure life out at a certain age or by reading a book or taking a class. We can simply see life as a journey by remaining curious, just like the little one within us, while also being kind and purposeful.

Here's what I want for you—to believe in your humble heart to do the "right" thing as it makes sense to you. At the end of the day, to go to bed and wake up living life in the most amazing, authentic, and fullest way possible. This is not a blasé way of living. This is and can be our real reality. Touch the earth fully and feel connected to this place, where you are, where you are understanding, where you are learning, and where you can see your part in the puzzle of life. See and feel the momentum of life and care about things equally as a caretaker of our precious earth. Try not to see this as a burden or an obligation on you, but rather you're a community member doing your part.

With love and appreciation, together we can contribute to the world by having a creative relationship with nature so that we live in a more harmonious place. We can also contribute to the world through our lineage, by embodying these practices and passing them down to others. If one day we see that we are not feeling in alignment, or we just don't care to be in alignment, we can just reach down and literally touch Mother Earth and ask for her support. She will be there at just the right time for you.

So, here we sit, dear reader. My hope for us is that we go off into our lives feeling more loved and more inspired than ever before. Lastly, remember that the garden of love is in your heart, not somewhere else outside of you, and being at one with every plant, insect, and animal is possible. We are all divine natural creatures, and when we are connected to our truest Self, we feel, express, and experience happier and more connected lives. This place already is within us and when we honor who we are, we honor those around us. May we anchor into this place daily by living in awareness and loving who we are, right where we are today.

All my love to you,
Mellara, xo

ACKNOWLEDGMENTS

Thank you to my gorgeous, loyal, and hardworking husband—you are my world. I love you and the life we are sharing together. I know that I am able to do so much of what I do because of your love and support. You are an ever-present grounding force in my life. You love me un-conditionally, take good care of me and the kids, and most of all, accept me for who I am. I am grateful to walk alongside you in this life.

Leela, my beautiful daughter, I couldn't imagine life without you. I love you more than words could say. Your joyful energy and gentle heart are contagious to be around. Our beach walks and window shopping are some of the most fun things to do in life. I am blessed to be your mommy. You are strong, and beyond capable, and I know that what-ever you set your mind and heart to do, you'll make it happen. My dear angel, thank you for being you.

Charlie, my one and only son, I love you. I pray that you continue to walk a path that is true to you. You continue to be who you are and share your light and creative heart with the lucky ones who get to be around you. You are generous, and kind, and I am fortunate to be your mom. You see things as they are and let me know it, and I am grateful for your honesty. I admire your creative ideas—keep up your excellent work and dedication to what matters most to you! You are an amazing human being.

Thank you, Jennifer Leigh Selig, my incredible publisher, and woman extraordinaire! I always love working with you and Mandorla Books. I know deeply that you have my best interest at heart and for that, I am eternally grateful. You are a woman's woman, yet probably it might be truer to say that you are so freaking cool and anyone would be blessed to work with you!

Naomi Boshari, my beautiful editor from across the pond. You are remarkable! Your trust in me and my book is evident. Your heart shines through every word you edit, and you have such grace and harmony about you. I couldn't be more grateful and happy that we worked together on this book. Thank you!

Lisa Carta, I cannot thank you enough for the most beautiful design of the front and back cover of this book. You are a true artist and one with heart. Thank you for your patience and kindness—it is always a joy and honor to work with you!

Arnie Kotler, I know we didn't work on this book together, but I wanted to take the opportunity to thank you (again) for our time together when you edited my first book, *A Life Worth Living*. I became the writer I am today because of our time together. I continue to feel gratitude in my heart for that and all of the writing gifts and support you have given me.

To my beloved readers before the book went to print, Sophia Colamarino (your eye for detail is out of sight), Mike Anzenberger, Suzy Dito, Sara Hoffa, Julie Young, Sarah Travis, Troy Brady, Karen Lieberman, and the one and only Carson Beckemeyer—you rock! I really would not have the book that I have today without your advice, suggestions, and support. You really held space for me when I needed it the most.

And finally, I would like to thank my yoga students, especially those who have been with me for so long. The responsibility I have as your teacher inspires me to accept the things that I cannot change, to show up fully, and to continue to learn.

And a deep bow of gratitude goes to all my teachers, formal and not. I love and appreciate what I have been given from you and sometimes just by being in your presence.

Lastly, I want to thank you, dear reader, for reading my book. I feel honored that you took the precious time to do so. Please be gentle with yourself and know that you matter. There is no one else in the world quite like you. Your presence and peaceful heart are what our world needs more of. Don't spend a single minute being hard on yourself. You are enough, beautiful, and absolutely exactly where you are supposed to be. Don't ever feel that your life is fated as every minute you are co-creating your reality with the Universe. We are here on this Earth school, as I like to call it, to make mistakes and learn from our experiences. So, keep being you and keep shining! The world needs your light.

ABOUT THE AUTHOR

Mellara Gold has been teaching meditation and mindful yoga for over two decades, influenced by the study of Hatha yoga, mindfulness, and Buddhism. She is the author of two books: *A Life Worth Living: A Journey of Self-Discovery Through Mindfulness, Yoga, and Living in Awareness,* and *Living in Awareness: Deepening Our Daily Lives Through Prayer, Ritual, and Meditation.* Mellara's inspirational style of teaching interweaves the physical and spiritual aspects of yoga, sharing primarily from the radiance of her own insights and the practice of self-inquiry.

Mellara was born in Queensland, Australia, and at the age of seventeen moved to Los Angeles to attend the prestigious Lee Strasberg Theatre Institute. After roles in *Don't Look Back,* with Peter Fonda (1996) and *Love Boat: The Next Wave* (1998), a depleting injury led her to embark on a healing journey, focusing on yoga. At the Center for Yoga and other Los Angeles studios, she immersed herself in Hatha, Iyengar, Viniyoga, Ashtanga, and other traditions, and completed teacher training with Erich Schiffmann and Saul David Raye.

After eighteen years teaching yoga in the U.S., Mellara returned to Australia to study for two years at the Uniting Awareness Centre, under the guidance of Channa Dassanayaka. She then moved back to California teaching online and in-person workshops, retreats, private sessions, and trainings. She now lives on the South Shore of Massachusetts with her husband, Mike, and children Leela and

Charlie, where she teaches and contributes regularly to *OM Yoga & Lifestyle Magazine*, *Elephant Journal*, and other lifestyle and spiritual magazines.

Mellara is available for private yoga, yogic breathing practices, meditation coaching, and spiritual & mindfulness counseling, with easy online booking in your time zone. Visit https://mellara.com/.

Photo of Mellara Gold by In Her Image Photography
www.inherimagephoto.com

Printed in Great Britain
by Amazon

23793308R00059